No DRY Season

Rod Parsley

No DRY Season

Charisma
HOUSE
A STRANG COMPANY

No Dry Season by Rod Parsley
Published by Charisma House
A Strang Company
600 Rinehart Road
Lake Mary, FL 32746
www.strangbookgroup.com

Unless otherwise noted, all Scripture quotations are from the King James Version of the Bible.

Scripture quotations marked The Message are from *THE MESSAGE.* Copyright © 1993, 1994, 1995. Used by permission of NavPress Publishing Group.

Scripture quotations marked NAS are from the New American Standard Bible. Copyright © 1960, 1962, 1963, 1968, 1971, 1972, 1973, 1975, 1977 by the Lockman Foundation. Used by permission.

Scripture quotations marked NIV are from the Holy Bible, New International Version. Copyright © 1973, 1978, 1984, International Bible Society. Used by permission.

Library of Congress Catalog Card Number: 96-71394
International Standard Book Number: 978-0-88419-464-4

09 10 11 12 13 – 21 20 19 18 17
Printed in the United States of America

D r. Lester Sumrall once told me that if you have two or three real friends during your life you are truly a rich man. Dr. Sumrall was my spiritual mentor, my pastor, my friend — a man of faith and destiny.

In April 1996 he said good-bye to this world, stepped across Jordan and went home to be with our precious Lord.

My first encounter with him was over fifteen years ago. Our church had only 180 people. When he came the building was packed, and we had folding chairs set up everywhere. The windows were open, and people sat on blankets outside. We had to set up his product table outside in the driveway because there was no room for it in our small building. He preached like a man from another world. I sat in awe and amazement at the inspired words that flowed out of his spirit.

After the service I took him to dinner and apologized for not being better prepared for him. I said, "Dr. Sumrall, I am just going to have to increase my faith and get a bigger place. Then when you come we can have room to accommodate the people, and your products won't get blown over by the wind."

In Dr. Sumrall's unique fashion he looked straight across the table at me with his baby-blue eyes and said, "Hmm. You don't need more faith."

I said, "No, sir, you are right. Thank you." My inexperience was sitting across the table from this man of great wisdom and experience.

He said, "What you need is to know what faith is."

"Yes, sir, I would like to know," I responded eagerly.

He answered, "Faith is simply knowing God."

Since that time we have shared many special moments which would take time and eternity to write down if I tried to tell what this man of God has meant to me and the tremendous impact he has had on my life and ministry. He protected me, guided me, instructed me, corrected me and exhorted me. He encouraged me and inspired me. He helped me to have a closer, deeper walk with God and increased my understanding of the spirit realm as no other human has ever done. I always looked forward to calling my pastor, just to hear him say, "Glory be to God!" We talked, walked, laughed, ate, cried, prayed and preached together.

Dr. Sumrall was a rare individual, a spiritual giant and one of the great patriarchs of faith. He tirelessly traveled the world, ministering to kings and presidents. He reached out with a loving heart and a helping hand to lost and hurting people all over the world.

He shaped the lives of multitudes of young ministers, equipping us to carry the fires of revival forward in this final outpouring of the Holy Spirit. He taught us the truths the Lord placed in his heart, and he did his best to pass on to us the wisdom and knowledge gained during his years in ministry.

But today I am faced with the reality that my pastor is no longer here. I cannot begin to put into words the emptiness in my heart since he passed on to glory. On more than one occasion I have found myself reaching for the phone to dial Dr. Sumrall's number just so I could hear his voice.

Our church building is dedicated as a memorial to the

man who was the friend of God, lover of souls and the enemy of hell. The hallway outside my office is lined with many pictures of our precious time together, each of which holds a story very dear to my heart. Even now I find it difficult to look at them because I know in this life I will never see him again. Dr. Sumrall was the perfect reflection of Jesus' truth, grace, boldness and tenderness. Heaven must be a reality because surely God has a place for a man like this.

So it is with this in mind, coupled with my deep love, respect and admiration for this man and his ministry, that this book is lovingly dedicated to his memory. May his anointing continue to be felt on earth, and may the effect of his work carry on until Jesus comes.

Dr. Sumrall, I will meet you at the gate of glory. Until then, as you taught me — I will remember to feed my faith and starve my doubts to death.

CONTENTS

Preface

No Dry Season!

No dry season! The warrior's temples pounded with the past promise. That word was all he had to hold onto as he made his way through the desert.

The sun had long ago beat down on the scorched earth, cracking the mud and creating fissures that plummeted deep and wide. The fractured soil now looked like lips parched from an endless dry season filled with only arid winds and empty clouds.

Looking toward the horizon the battle-weary warrior crossed a sea of dunes and gazed desperately at the morning sky hoping to see...

just a glimmer,
   just a shimmer,
      just a spot,

just a dot,
    just one cloud filled with
    the promise of moisture.

How the warrior would welcome just a drop of dew on his thirsty lips! Fading memories of rain fleetingly crossed his vision as mirages. When he had started this journey, everything was new, fresh and filled with hope. Not distinguished by birth or ancestry, this standard bearer had been adopted into the Captain's ranks. He had discovered in following the Captain that there was life after birth and joy in the midst of trials and tests.

In the beginning rain fell daily and water was abundant. The Captain's standard bearer never thirsted and never experienced a dry season. But the enemy initiated unrelenting attacks against the warrior, driving him further and further away from the abundant lands to the sparsely planted plains and then into the desert. What had been rivers diminished into a brook, which finally trickled into oblivion.

Worn, tired, discouraged and hopeless,
    the once mighty warrior,
        standard bearer to the Captain of the hosts,
            stumbled aimlessly through the wilderness.

A season of dryness had overtaken him like a twister kicking up searing sand that blistered the body and parched the soul. The overcomer had been overcome.

How had it happened? Explanations never tell all the story or explain all the contributing causes. Nonetheless, the dry season could have been forecast.

First, the warrior standard bearer had wandered away from his Captain. Why? The loud voices competing for the soldier's attention had drowned out the still, small voice of his Commander. He could no longer hear the Captain's directions.

Then, communication ceased. Oh, communion was not broken all at once. But the long walks and talks together had turned into rushed encounters from which the standard bearer quickly excused himself before the Captain could reply. Mistakenly, the warrior had believed that reports about the enemy's movements was more important than listening to his Leader's vision and heart.

Finally, the standard bearer lost his way. Infrequent contact with his Commander had caused him to look for signposts in the surrounding world. Detours offered exciting promises of quick fixes and instant success. Battles were no longer fought but avoided. The enemy's proposals of cease-fires and truces made it easier to hold on to safe ground rather than to risk fighting for new territory.

What happened? A dry season swept into the standard bearer's life. Yet in spite of the absence of rain, the lack of cool breezes and the numbing darkness that welled up inside of him, the warrior held fast to the promise.

No Dry Season!

Like a pickpocket in a crowded subway station who worked with ease when the lights went out, the enemy had plundered what rightfully belonged to the standard bearer, and the warrior had lost hope. Succumbing to the lies of the desert, he curled up in a fetal position to face what he believed to be his last night in the desert. *Tomorrow will not come for me,* he thought. *I will die in the night.*

Nightmares flooded the wounded soldier's restless slumber. Past hurts resurfaced as troubled dreams:

A broken marriage,
   a rebellious child,
      a lost job,
         a wounded spirit,
            a financial crash,
               a friend's rejection,

a shattered hope,
an untimely tragedy....

All through the night, the crushed standard bearer traded his shield for fiery darts,
his protection for vulnerability,
his forgiveness for guilt,
his hopes for despair,
and his restoration for abandonment.

Then, the faintest fingers of light grabbed hold of night's murky veil, parting its dark curtains and revealing an approaching host on the horizon. Hoping against all hope, the warrior lifted a storm-beaten face toward the East and peered through the night into the morning sky.

"Who is she who looketh forth as the morning..." (Song 6:10). *I am still alive,* thought the warrior. *I still have breath. Much has been lost or stolen, but within my bones a fire still burns. I can still look out and see light. Darkness flees at the mention of my Captain's name.*

"Fair as the moon..." (Song 6:10). *I am not who the world says I am. The silver screen's portrait of me as...*
a bound-up woman,
a victimized child,
an irresponsible man,
an elderly castoff,
a compulsive addict,
a driven workaholic,
an insatiable consumer,
a promiscuous pleasure-seeker,
is a lie.

I can reject the world and its endless wastelands filled with deceptive mirages.

"Clear as the sun..." (Song 6:10). The wavy images of the approaching hosts begin to come into focus. *I can see only*

14

one figure clearly amidst the thundering masses approaching out of dawn's early light. Night dissolves with His returning. *I can turn my back on the night and* repent *of its shadowy lusts and passions. I can stand again. I feel a wind of* refreshing *blowing across my brow. I sense* restoration *coming into my dead bones. I see flowers blooming in the desert and springs of living water bubbling out of the dry land. My Captain, the lover of my soul, is* returning *for me. I must get ready!*

"Terrible as an army with banners?" (Song 6:10). *Now my thoughts clear and my queries receive their answers.* She *who looks out from the night into the morning is the church. She is you and me marching terrible as an army with banners.*

As you pick up this book and skim through its pages, ask yourself:

- Has any of this warrior's journey been your own?

- Have you retreated to the sidelines, afraid to face life's challenges?

- Are you believing the lies of the enemy about your past, present and future?

- Do you find yourself shadowboxing with demonic powers instead of possessing the promises of God?

- Are you simply "holding down the fort," afraid to risk everything for the Captain of the hosts?

- Do you need to *repent* of your past, be *refreshed* in your spiritual walk, claim the *restoration* that your Commander has already won for you on the cross, and get ready with bold anticipation for His *return?*

This book is written for the faint of heart,
    the secret dwellers of the night,
        those hiding behind weak excuses

and crippling failure,
    the afflicted victims who hang at the rear
        every time the infantry column advances.

It is also written for those strong and brave,
    whose bones burn with a fire for the Lord,
        who zealously labor in the harvest,
            and who are raising high the standard and
            lifting up the banner of Christ.

Your morning has come. A cloud the size of a man's hand is rising on the horizon. Laden with wind, rain and fire, it is gathering above you. Glory and honor will crown your life while signs and wonders will follow you into the four corners of the earth.

No dry season. God is calling you to raise high the standard for living in this final generation. The time has come to plant your flag, possess the land, raise the standard and march under the banner of the King of kings.

Your time as a standard bearer for the King has arrived. The heavens are opening. The wind of the Holy Spirit is blowing. Holy fire is consuming all that is dross and refining all that is gold. The latter and the former rains are falling. You will reap before the sower's seed hits the ground.

This book will equip you to raise high the standard, to experience the blessings of kingdom living and to march "terrible as an army with banners" who is winning this final generation to Jesus Christ.

Come with me out of your dry season and into the living waters flowing from the very throne of God. Declare to the enemy:

No dry season!
In Christ,
I raise high the standard for living
in the final generation.

1

The Standard
Has Been Passed On

The citizens of heaven sit on the edges of their seats. As if viewing a thrilling suspense story, they peer through the portals of eternity onto the stages of time to witness the final scene of the human drama. The curtain has risen on the final act. Will the lead actor rise to the occasion? All the years of apprenticeship are over. It's time to unveil the character of the lead player.

The end of this eternal drama for the hearts and souls of humanity rests with us. Throughout the ages saints have journeyed through wildernesses, crossed deserts, faced hostile animals and governments and sacrificed their lives so we might have this moment in spiritual history. The call to bring in the harvest, win the battle and possess the land rests with us — the final generation. To us the sword has been passed. In this hour we are anointed to raise high the standard of Jesus Christ and proclaim the gospel with Pentecostal power.

The sword of God's Word and the anointing of His power were handed to me and this generation by my spiritual father, Dr. Lester Sumrall. That sword had been handed to him by a fiery, Holy Spirit-baptized, miracle-working evangelist named Smith Wigglesworth.

My former pastor, Dr. Lester Sumrall, lived or preached in more than one hundred nations. He spoke to more preachers in a year than any other man I knew. Dr. Sumrall was an historian as well as a theologian, missionary, statesmen and author. He fulfilled the five-fold ministry office gifts as completely as any person I have observed. Oral Roberts called him the greatest living patriarch of God.

As a teacher, Dr. Sumrall wrote more than 150 books and study guides that people in many nations are still using today. As a pastor he shepherded both his congregation in South Bend, Indiana, and hundreds of pastors from around the world who looked to him for counsel, wisdom, understanding, discernment and direction. Tirelessly, he traveled the globe as an evangelist seeking to save the lost. He saw them slipping over the brink of hell from every nation, tribe and tongue. He felt their blood was on his hands, so he traveled constantly, taking the gospel to the four corners of the earth. As a prophet he heard from God and imparted vision and direction to the church of Jesus Christ.

> **We are anointed by the Holy Spirit to be the standard-bearers in this generation.**

Space does not permit me to tell you all that he did and

all that he meant to me. He pastored me and hundreds of others pastors, becoming an apostle to us for the planting of the gospel throughout the earth. As God's apostle, he was one of hell's greatest enemies in the twentieth century.

Dr. Sumrall lived in covenant with God. At seventeen, dying of tuberculosis, spitting up chunks of his lungs onto a pillow, a choice confronted him. His doctor had already signed his death certificate, remarking as he did so, "He'll be dead by morning." That lie was uttered over seventy-five years ago. That young man — a standard bearer for God — long outlived his doctor.[1]

What happened that destiny-filled night in Lester Sumrall's room as he lay dying on his bed? What choice faced him? In a vision God showed him a Bible and a casket. A voice thundered, "Choose! If you embrace the Bible and preach the gospel, I will let you live. But if you don't, that will be your casket." Young Lester chose the Bible. He took the sword. He lifted high the banner! He became God's mighty general for his generation.

From Dr. Sumrall, other young preachers and I received that piercing sword and a powerful anointing to raise the standard and lift high the banner of Jesus Christ. My God, what a responsibility! Take notice: Both you and I have been called to be standard bearers.

God is depending upon each one of us to proclaim His message to a hurting and dying world. Christ has commissioned us. The Holy Spirit has anointed us. I am a standard bearer, and so are you! All of us must lift high God's banner.

How do we respond? We are awed. We are humbled. We are astounded. We are anointed by the Holy Spirit to be the standard bearers in this generation.

Let me tell you about those standard bearers who have gone before us. They carried the sword. They walked and ministered in the power of the anointing. They were the standard bearers for us.

Smith Wigglesworth

My former pastor received the sword from a rough, uneducated plumber turned evangelist, Smith Wigglesworth, who was born in 1859 in Menston, Yorkshire, England. Wigglesworth decided to follow Christ in a Wesleyan Methodist meeting at the age of eight. Later his wife, Polly, took up the banner before Smith did. She evangelized her community through a little mission in Bradford, England. Her husband helped her but did not answer the call of God until the age of forty-seven.

> I bless you with all the faith that is within me. I give to you all that God has given to me. I return it all to God through you.

In 1907, halfway through his life, the Holy Spirit fell on Smith Wigglesworth at a revival in Sunderland, England. It was then that God's anointing knocked him down, baptized him in the fire of the Holy Spirit with evidence of speaking in other tongues, and raised him up to be a standard bearer for his generation. Preaching around the world, Smith Wigglesworth saw thousands saved, healed and delivered. He went home to be with the Lord in 1947. But before he died, Wigglesworth passed on the mantle of his anointing to my dear pastor, Dr. Lester Sumrall.

In the late 1930s Dr. Sumrall and Smith Wigglesworth developed a deep and lasting friendship. After Wigglesworth first heard Dr. Sumrall preach, he said to him, "Come see me anytime."

Dr. Sumrall did just that. He visited Smith Wigglesworth every other week or so for over two years. Wigglesworth was in his giving years. While he was with him, Sumrall would sit attentively, looking up into Wigglesworth's face as he listened to the wisdom from his many years of experience in the work of the Lord. The two men loved each other in the Lord. Dr. Sumrall told how they would hug and then share with one another for hours on end.

On one visit to Wigglesworth, Dr. Sumrall showed up with a newspaper tucked under his arm. Brother Wigglesworth answered the door and asked, "What's that?"

Sumrall answered, "It's a newspaper."

"You'll have to leave that outside," Wigglesworth instructed. "I don't allow that to come into my home." Smith Wigglesworth had no other book in his home except a Bible. It was all he would read or allow anyone else to read in his home.

In 1939, as the war mounted in Europe, the British government asked all the foreign civilians to leave the country.

Dr. Sumrall received an official notice that he must leave, but before he did, he paid one final visit to Brother Wigglesworth. As he entered the house, Sumrall said to Wigglesworth, "Dear Brother, I won't see you anymore. The government has told me I must leave the country. I'm sorry that I must come and say good-bye." Both men stood facing each other for a moment. Brother Sumrall bowed his head over onto Smith's chest. Wigglesworth wrapped his arms around Sumrall and began to tremble and weep. He pronounced: I bless you with all the faith that is within me. I give to you all that God has given to me. I return it all to God through you.

Tears streamed from Wigglesworth's uplifted face and poured down to anoint Dr. Sumrall's bowed head. He prayed at length a great blessing over Sumrall. Then Wigglesworth grabbed his shoulders and shouted, "I see it!"

"What do you see?" asked Dr. Sumrall.

With eyes fixed on God, Wigglesworth declared, "There is a revival coming, the likes of which the world has never seen. I see hospitals empty. All the patients are running down the street and their doctors are running after them. Everybody is healed by the power of God. I see every kind of cripple healed."

"You do?" inquired Sumrall.

"I do," responded Wigglesworth. "I won't live to see it, but you will live to see it."

Wigglesworth was in his giving years. Dr. Sumrall was in his receiving years. He received from Smith Wigglesworth the sword, the banner, the standard to raise high for Christ.

Remember Alexander the Great? After conquering the world he lay on his deathbed as a young man. Calling his four mighty generals to his bedside, Alexander divided the world among them. He passed on the sword. He handed over the banner.

> In the last season of our lives, the season of giving, we give away all that we have to the next generation so they may reap the harvest from our labor.

In the same way, God's mighty conqueror — Smith Wigglesworth — passed on the sword of God's anointing to Dr. Sumrall. If he had not given it away, it could have gone to the grave with him.

Smith Wigglesworth spent his life sowing into the lives of those around him. Then, at the giving time in his life, he sowed a powerful anointing into the life of Lester Sumrall. It was time for the next generation to carry the banner on, to raise the standard high. It was time for Sumrall to take the sword.

Different seasons take place in our lives. As we move out of dry seasons, God moves us into seasons of giving, serving

22

and receiving. First, we find ourselves in a season of receiving. During this season we are learning all we can from great men and women of God. Then we move into a season of serving. We sow from daylight to dark and sometimes into the night for a harvest of lost souls. Much of the harvest we will never reap; others will. In the last season of our lives, the season of giving, we give away all that we have to the next generation so they may reap the harvest from our labor. They will be in their season of receiving. They will reap a harvest they have not sown for the glory of God's kingdom.

If the Lord tarries, every person in life must eventually hand his or her sword to another. It was so with Dr. Lester Sumrall. After decades of serving God and working hard to sow the harvest Sumrall turned to me and to our generation to hand over his sword. He passed on the years of Smith Wigglesworth's anointing to this generation. Now we are the ones called to lift up the banner. We are the ones called to raise the standard of God in our world for this generation.

Receiving the Sword from Dr. Sumrall

Just as Dr. Lester Sumrall had a spiritual father in Smith Wigglesworth, I had a spiritual father in Dr. Sumrall. During our relationship over the years, I sometimes would think to myself, *What would the world be like without Dr. Sumrall?* I wouldn't want to think that thought. He stood immovable in God for over sixty years of ministry.

I would remember how Dr. Sumrall had lived or preached in more than one hundred nations of the world. I would think of the time in the Bilibid prison in the Philippines when he cast a devil out of one girl. Her healing resulted in a harvest of 150,000 Filipino adults who gave their lives to Christ. One of the largest churches in the Orient is there today as a result of his faithfulness.

Sumrall was a father in the faith to me just as Smith Wigglesworth was to him. In the lonely times he was there for me. When the pressures were too great to bear, all I had to do was call him and hear the Lord say through him, "Everything's going to be all right."

I loved him more than words could ever express. I remember that while in Jerusalem in 1987, Dr. Sumrall summoned Ulf Ekman of Sweden and me to his room. As we stepped off the elevator and turned the corner to walk down the hall to his room, we stopped dead in our tracks. At that moment the Holy Spirit caused tears to well up in our eyes. We took each other by the hand, and I said, "We are at a moment of destiny." God spoke to me, "When you step through that door, you step through the threshold of destiny." So we prayed before we went into the room.

When we entered, Dr. Sumrall, the prophet of God, was sitting at a little table. Tears began to drip off his cheeks as he slid toward me a paper with the vision he had been writing for five hours, a vision of the *End Time Joseph Feed the Hungry Program*. I began to read the words that had been given from the heart of God when He had stirred my pastor from sleep at ten minutes before midnight the night before. God had said, "It is midnight prophetically, and it is almost time for Me to come. I care that My people do not starve to death before I come in the rapture of the church."

Since that time, literally hundreds of thousands of Christians around the world have received millions of pounds of food transported on mighty ships and a mammoth Hercules C-130 cargo aircraft. Thousands have given their lives to Jesus Christ through the great crusades and revivals as the Bread of life was ministered. Pastors from nearly every nation have been trained to be a part of this global feeding program.

I was with this great man of God in so many different situations and witnessed God's mighty power. Personally, I was touched through the many phone calls and visits during which he counseled me and shared the things of God. He was constantly telling me stories of his travels with great men of God, not only Smith Wigglesworth, but also men like Howard Carter, who led my pastor around the world and taught him revelation knowledge about the nine gifts of the Spirit.

Dr. Sumrall once told the story of a time when Brother Carter's Bible school was in need of money to pay bills. Because of World War II, the school had been hit particularly hard. Brother Carter believed God for the money, and the exact amount needed for the bills arrived in a brown paper bag. He told Dr. Sumrall that it was "only just enough to pay the bills." From Howard Carter my pastor had learned the important lesson that we are not to depend on man but only on God to supply our needs. He imparted his anointing into Dr. Sumrall's life like Brother Wigglesworth had.

Dr. Sumrall performed the ceremony at which my beautiful wife, Joni, and I were wed. He dedicated both of our children, Ashton and Austin, to the Lord. For years he and I had walked together, talked together, laughed and cried together, lost and conquered together. The Spirit of the Lord had knit our hearts together as one.

I was asked to preach his lovely wife's funeral. After the service Dr. Sumrall looked at me with tears streaming down his face and said, "Mama is the only woman I ever kissed in my life." He was eighty-three and was married to the same woman for almost fifty years. He remained forever faithful to his Lord and his wife. So often he would say to me, "Rod, it's not hard to live right."

At Sumrall's own funeral I had to face the reality that I had lost my spiritual father. I asked myself during the service, *What are we going to do?* Then I got more personal. *What am I going to do?* The man who had passed the sword of God's anointing on to me had just gone to heaven. No alcohol or tobacco had ever touched his lips. He was a man of great spiritual authority, godly intensity, moral integrity and physical purity. My heart cried out, "What am I going to do?"

As I looked into his casket, the Holy Spirit answered my cry, "You are going to raise the standard." In other words, God was telling me to take the intensity up a notch, to guard *my* heart and my moral integrity and to flow more deeply in wisdom, purity and the anointing. God's call intensified: "Raise the standard!"

My mind went back to the night, not long before he died and joined his beloved Savior, when Dr. Sumrall passed on the sword to us. In our church service on November 26, 1992, Dr. Sumrall said:

> I have had young men run up to me and ask me to lay my hands on them and pass on the anointing I received from Smith Wigglesworth. But I say to them, "You haven't been with me. I was with Brother Wigglesworth for two years before he passed on the anointing." I never asked Wigglesworth to bless me. I was ready to leave simply by shaking hands. He chose to lay his hands on me because of what was in his heart. I could never pass on the sword to someone I did not know.
>
> God's power is not cheap. Many do not have it. They won't pay the price for it. Remember Joshua served Moses for forty years before Moses passed on the sword to him.
>
> I have known so many of the great men of the Pentecostal movement personally. Many of them left no junior behind them. You have no right to die until you leave a successor for yourself. So

many times those who have had amazing experiences have taken them to the grave. We miss a treasure when that happens. We must get all we can from God, use it to our greatest ability and then pass it on.

I believe that God's spiritual leadership in this country can be blessed by those who have had experiences, who have gone through the valley. They have something to share. You don't have to fall into the same pits that they have fallen into. You don't have to face the same problems they have had to face. You can receive from them how to go around some of the difficulties. More than that, a leader can give to you of the Holy Spirit that's within him. I give to you my spirit, my Holy Spirit. What's in my spirit I deliver to you. If all of us started doing that we would have a better world.

> Whatever anointings the Lord may have put on my life; whatever vision of saving the world; whatever vision in my heart; it will burn as bright or brighter in his heart.

Howard Carter told me many times, "Lester, you can't begin at the bottom. You have to begin where I leave off." If our older brethren would have us start where they finished instead of where they began, we would go further. Hallelujah!

I don't know how much longer I will live on planet earth. So now, I would like for Pastor Rod Parsley to come and his beautiful wife, Joni. We have never done a dual situation like this before, but we wish to do one right now. We wish to pass the sword to the new generation. I have behind me two swords. I have a military sword. It has been used in war. The other is a parading sword, but it has not been in battle. I am going to set it aside for now.

In the world of the spirit, I wish to pass the sword of apostleship to these who are here. The fruit of it is being born all over the earth. Nations are being blessed because of the ministry going out from here. Spiritual leadership goes out from here to the ends of the earth.

You heard Rod say that our attachment is very strong, and that it is. When he has a problem, I have a problem. I don't lose the problem. It stays with me day and night. Why? Because there is an attachment of the spirit inside.

I wish at this moment for all that may be in my spirit and my heart to pass to him. Whatever anointings the Lord may have put on my life; whatever vision of saving the world; whatever vision in my heart; it will burn as bright or brighter in his heart.

So leaving the parading sword to one side, I use the militant sword that went through the groaning and the crying of battle. I believe that it represents the passing of something from an elder who has been in the ministry sixty-three years to a younger who is reaching forward so strongly. We wish to pass the sword along to the pastor of this church and his wife. In the name of the Father, the Son and the Holy Spirit, putting your hands on it, I present to you this sword.

I believe that this will be a night we will all

remember. I believe it will be a night that God's holy anointing will increase and that even the healing power will be evident. In Jesus' name. And this beautiful companion [Joni], so compatible, will be blessed. Receive now.

At that moment, Dr. Sumrall touched us, and the power of the Holy Spirit fell upon on us. He and the congregation prayed over us as the sword was passed. The standard and banner of one generation was passed on to the next.

The Sword Is Passed on to You

That night with Dr. Sumrall was for me and my generation. That includes you! We are reaping a great harvest that was sown by the generation before us. We are a reaper generation. Because men of God like Smith Wigglesworth and Dr. Lester Sumrall have sown into the harvest fields, then handed over to us the banner and the standard of Christ, we are reaping where we have not sown. God's Word is being fulfilled in our midst:

> Behold, the days come, saith the Lord, that the plowman shall overtake the reaper, and the treader of grapes him that soweth seed; and the mountains shall drop sweet wine, and all the hills shall melt (Amos 9:13).

There is a fire burning within me to share how you can take the sword and become a standard bearer for this generation. I want you to move out of the dry season in your life and move into a season of refreshing and restoration.

As you read the coming pages, you will:

- Come out of the dry season in your life and experience the wonderful, refreshing river of God flowing out of you and blessing others.

- Discover how to raise high God's standard and banner in your life and in your world.

- Uncover and repent of the sin that keeps you from raising high His standard.

- Experience the reviving and refreshing of God in your life and be restored and made ready for Jesus' return.

- Hear the challenge and heed the call to wholeness, war, worship and warning.

I have God's sword in my hand to pass on to you. I have God's banner to deliver to you. I have God's standard for you to raise in your life. I want you to reap where you have not sown and become a mighty standard bearer for the kingdom of God.

Pray. Get ready for a supernatural breakthrough spiritually and physically in every area of your life. I believe a fresh anointing of God's Spirit will be poured out on you, and I believe God for you to:

- Drink in the rain from the Holy Spirit which will help to quench the insatiable thirst of your soul and spirit.

- Receive and learn all that you need to be His standard bearer.

- Serve and labor in His harvest.

- Give and pass on the sword of the anointing to this final generation.

I trust God that you will be transformed by the prophetic truths revealed in this book so that He can use you to stand and declare the gospel message to your family, your church and the world.

2

Raise High God's Standard

During the War of 1812, the ship Francis Scott Key was on was detained from leaving the waters near Baltimore. Looking across the bay in the Baltimore harbor, he could see Fort McHenry in the distance. It was September 13, 1814. As the night fell and light waned, suddenly the smoke of cannons and the burst of bombs lit the sky.

The screams of the war's dying filled the night. Francis Scott Key could hear the shouts of victims and the howl of missiles piercing the air, but no sound gave a clue as to who was winning and who was losing. Only the morning light would reveal the battle's outcome.

As darkness gave way to light, Francis Scott Key wrote on the back of an envelope,

O say, can you see, by the dawn's early light,
What so proudly we hailed at the twilight's last
   gleaming?
Whose broad stripes and bright stars, through the
   perilous fight,
O'er the ramparts we watched, were so gallantly
   streaming!
And the rockets' red glare, the bombs bursting in
   air,

She is the church within a church. The kingdom within a kingdom. The people of God within a people. The living water within a desert.

Gave proof through the night that our flag was still there:
O say, does that star-spangled banner yet wave
O'er the land of the free and the home of the brave?

The standard, the banner, the flag of our country waved gallantly in the morning breeze declaring for all to see that our army had withstood the attack and repelled the enemy. Every American should be proud to lift the banner of our country and declare that we are the land of the free and the home of the brave.

As Christians, you and I have a banner to lift, a flag to wave and a standard to raise high for all the world to see. Who are we to fly a banner? Whom do we serve and lift high as our standard? How can those living in a dry and thirsty land receive good news about the refreshing of God?

Who Is She That Looketh Forth as the Morning?

Who is she that looketh forth as the morning,

fair as the moon,
clear as the sun, and
terrible as an army with banners? (Song 6:10).

The Bible has much to say about banners and standards — flags, if you will. This passage declares that a terrible, mighty army marches under God's banner. Who is she?

Not everyone who shows up for church on Sunday morning to go through the rigors of religiosity and march to the cadences and creeds of men is she. She is the church within a church. The kingdom within a kingdom. The people of God within a people. The living water within a desert.

A remnant church called: terrible as an army with banners.

There is a problem in America. Yes, we may raise a national flag or banner at our sporting events and political rallies. Nonetheless, within the hearts of many who stand under that banner exists confusion, a lack of vision and a wavering commitment to our nation's standard.

There is a problem in the church. We, too, are having difficulty seeing our standard. We need to fix our eyes on the banner of Christ over us because we are to be a terrible army — terrorists, in fact. The army with banners is a terror to the forces of darkness and the alien armies of the Antichrist, which are arrayed against the body of Christ. The enemy is marching against the Lord Jesus Christ and against his anointed standard bearers, the church.

"Who is she that looketh forth as the morning...?" What does this scripture mean? It refers to the attitude of the church toward itself. Too often we find ourselves looking backward into the night instead of marching forward into the morning. Too often we find ourselves willing to endure dryness rather than declaring, *no dry season* in our lives. It is time for us to start living in the light of day. It is time for us to start living where the atmosphere of expectancy,

drenched with the moisture from heaven, rains down, soaking the soil of hope and creating a breeding ground for miracles.

Oh, there is no time like the dawning — no matter how sultry the night has been, no matter how dark. "Joy cometh in the morning" (Ps. 30:5).

You may be walking through the driest, darkest, most desperate situation of your life, but hold on — joy comes in the morning. Remember, weeping lasts only for a night. The church doesn't march in the night. The army of God goes forth in the morning and marches under the banner of light. Leave your night behind. Raise high the banner of Christ and march with the army of light.

Our Commander Himself declares, "I am the light of the world" (John 9:5). We march under the banner of light. Christ as the true light invades the darkness, and darkness cannot overcome His light. The Word proclaims, "In him [Christ] was life; and the life was the light of men. And the light shineth in darkness; and the darkness comprehended it not" (John 1:4-5).

Jesus also declares, "But whosoever drinketh of the water that I shall give him shall never thirst; but the water that I shall give him shall be in him a well of water springing up into everlasting life" (John 4:14). Stop drinking from the old wells of your past traditions and worldly preoccupations. Refuse to drink the stagnant, sin-infested, putrid waters of this world and dig new wells deep into the waters of God.

Sing a new song unto the Lord as Israel did: "Then Israel sang this song, Spring up, O well; sing ye unto it" (Num. 21:17). Christ is the well of living water springing up within us.

How can we claim a promise of no more dry seasons in our lives? We must allow His well to flow continually and eternally from within us through the Holy Spirit. "He that believeth on me [Jesus], as the scripture hath said, out of his belly shall flow rivers of living water. (But this spake he of the Spirit, which they that believe on him should receive)" (John 7:38-39).

Go forward with a church which gets up with the morning light and walks in the former and latter rains of God. Remember, no matter how hot the night has been, the dawn is always accompanied by a cool, moist breeze. It will cool your fevered brow. A fresh breeze of God's Spirit is issuing forth today over the sapphire sill of heaven's gate for those who raise high the standard of Jesus Christ. Those under His banner are rejoicing every morning as they rise up saying, "This is the day which the Lord hath made; we will rejoice and be glad in it" (Ps. 118:24). The greatest day, the greatest dawn, the greatest morning that the church has ever seen lies straight ahead.

People have commented to me, "Brother Wigglesworth told Brother Sumrall that he himself wouldn't see revival but that Brother Sumrall would. So, where is the revival?" My response has been, "Under what banner are you marching, my friend? Open your eyes. Get under the blessing and the standard of the most high God. The revival isn't coming; it's here!"

Wigglesworth never saw crowds of people like we see today around the world who are hearing the gospel preached in stadiums, on television and in the streets. Just one of my messages beamed around the world by television is seen in 136 nations of the world. Revival is here!

Blind eyes are opened. Not just in America, but in China, Argentina, South Africa, Korea and in scores of other nations around the world, revival is breaking forth as the morning. My own mother was healed of breast cancer. The doctors said on a Tuesday, "Your mother has breast cancer. We must operate and remove her right breast on Thursday."

We said, "You can't. We have to go to a missionary convention on Wednesday."

The doctor responded, "I won't be responsible for what happens."

"You won't have to be," we replied. "We have another One who is responsible. His name is Jehovah-Rapha. He is the God that healeth thee." Today my mother is completely and totally healed of cancer and is preaching the saving, healing, delivering gospel of Jesus Christ around the world.

> God's banner miraculously changes all those who march under it. His standard transforms and refreshes all those who raise it. Raise the standard of Christ and be changed!

You may say, "Brother Rod, I haven't experienced that kind of revival." Then come out of the night. Get into the light. Find a people of God who are lifting high the banner of Christ. Raise the standard and revival will come to your life, chasing all darkness and night back to hell's door.

Fair as the Moon

In Palestine I've seen the moon hanging in the sky while the sun is still dawning. Both sun and moon share celestial beauty. The moon is significant only as she fulfills her purpose in reflecting the light, energy and glory of the sun. As we march under His banner, we reflect His light and glory. This is how the world sees Christ reflected in us.

Genesis 1:27 declares that God created us in His own image. The word *image* refers to "a reflection." We are the moon to the Son of light. The moon has no ability to shine on her own. Those under His banner have no persona, no personality, no ability, no talent and no power on their own to dispel the darkness. Like Moses, we must go to the mountain of God to receive the light of His glory. His face shone with God's glory, not his own (see Ex. 34:29-35).

God is able as our banner, our standard, to do exceedingly abundantly in us above all that we can imagine or think (see Eph. 3:20). The anointing of the bride — the church — is to go forth as the morning and to be like the moon — reflecting the awesome light and glory of the bridegroom, Jesus Christ.

I'm tired of a weak and feeble army of saltless saints going into the world marching under every banner and running after every flag that comes along. We vainly try to reflect the crumbling creeds, the deadly denominationalism, the ruinous relativism of this world's systems. No light is in them. No power exists outside of *the* Light. Stop running after every man, every new program, every method, every television offer of cheap grace that brings you a fleeting burst of excitement.

Stop running around after every false flicker of light and instead plant yourself under the standard of the true light of Jesus Christ. Be what the Bible ordains you to become. "But we all, with open face beholding as in a glass the glory of the Lord, are changed into the same image from glory to glory, even as by the Spirit of the Lord" (2 Cor. 3:18).

God's banner miraculously changes all those who march under it. His standard transforms and refreshes all those who raise it. Raise the standard of Christ and be changed!

Like the moon reflects the sun, you are to mirror the Son, Jesus Christ, and drive away all darkness. An old proverb says we must "light a candle to curse the darkness." Shelve that saying! Rather, burn with the blazing banner of Christ and chase the darkness back into the shadows of night.

Clear as the Sun

Before you know it, the moon has slipped over the bosom of the morning, and the dawn has risen to dominate the sky. The sun continues to escalate in meridian glory until it now stands at full noon, blazing high in the clear sky. This is how we should respond to Him who created us.

Would to God that we could find a church which would be clear as the sun! Oh that we might become completely transparent to God so that a dying world could see His light without a shadow of distortion!

Desiring to shine like the Son of light, the church needs to cry out, "It is not the deacon, it's not the elder, it's not the preacher, it's not the singer, it's not the choir, but it's me — it's me, O God, standing in the need of prayer."

Becoming clear as the sun requires us first to become clean as the fresh fallen snow. "Though your sins be as scarlet, they shall be as white as snow" (Is. 1:18).

What keeps us from raising high the standard of Christ?
   What hinders our going forth into the morning?
      What shadows fall on our reflection, keeping us from being as fair as the moon?
         What blocks the radiant light so we fail to be as clear as the sun?

Sin! Unconfessed, unrepented, unrelenting sin stops the church and scatters the saints of God. You may be unable to raise the standard right now where you are. Why?

- Sin shackles your walk.

- Sin blocks your well.

- Sin corrupts your anointing.

- Sin breaks off the ax head.

You may be like the man cutting wood when his ax broke and the ax head fell into the water. He cried out, "Alas, master! for it was borrowed" (2 Kin. 6:5). No longer can you do the work. No longer can you fight the battle. No longer can you march in the army and raise high the banner. At some point in your life, your ax broke. Sin snapped you in two. When did sin shackle your life?

Looking into the murky waters of past sin, you may be able to point to the spot where it happened. Point to the spot now and confess:

- Right there is where I surrendered to sin.

- Right there is where I started drinking from old wells of tradition and religion.

- Right there is where I stopped praying and praising Him.

- Right there is where I stopped reading my Bible.

- Right there is where I compromised the truth.

- Right there is where impurity stained my purity.

- Right there is where I stopped confessing God's Word.

Now, stop pointing to the sin and start pointing to the Savior. Stop crawling around in the pigpen and start washing in the living water of Jesus. Cry out, "Here I am, God, standing in the need of prayer. Here I am, God, standing in the need of You!"

The time has come for you to come clean with God. Get washed by the blood. Become transparent before God, clear as the sun, and He will shine through you. The ax head will begin to float, miracles will start to happen, and your power to raise the standard will be restored.

Terrible as an Army With Banners

Now don't be shocked. Stay with me on this point. Get ready. God saved the best revelation in Song of Solomon 6:10 for last. Going forth as the morning, out of the night and away from the darkness, isn't the end. It is only the beginning.

Reflecting the light of Christ — becoming fair as the moon — takes us only so far. Reflection may be beautiful, but it's not powerful. There's more!

Becoming clear as the sun makes us transparent so that others may see Christ in us and through us. Being clear as the sun lets the light shine through once the sin has been washed from our lives. Yet, even this isn't the best for us. To raise the standard, we must be willing to go even further with God. As a terrible army lifting high our banners, we must respond to the enemies of the cross.

I am challenging you to raise the standard. The battle is about to begin with more ferocity and terrible fighting than you and I have ever experienced. I know that you may not want me to tell you this, and neither does the devil. But I am crawling into his caves and tunnels to dig him out and expose him to the light.

Some may protest that the church *has* raised the standard and fought the battle. I am not convinced. We have so lowered biblical standards, so compromised God's absolute truth, so watered down His anointing, so polluted the well, streams and river of God, that we are aiming at what used to be beneath our feet. With no standards to look up to, we look down — bowed and defeated — marching like sheep to the slaughter. I cry with Isaiah, "Truth is fallen in the street" (59:14).

What am I talking about? We live in a microwave society which is constantly looking for immediate gratification. Moral decay eats away at the very fabric of our lives. The church has become so worldly and the world so churchy that it is hard to tell the difference. Prayerlessness has replaced praying and interceding through the night. Waiting for God has been abandoned as we rush headlong into off-beat human schemes that lead nowhere.

The temptation to withdraw from church into isolation is strong. But I refuse to join the masses. I, for one, am going to raise the standard of Jesus Christ against the devil, against shepherds who fleece their flocks, against sheep who run with wolves instead of rushing headlong into the Good Shepherd's sheepfold. Pastor, raise the standard of Christ with me. Teacher, usher, elder, deacon and saint, fly the flag. It's time to become the terrible, awesome army of God and to march with banners — His standards — into the fray!

March Under Jehovah-Nissi

The Bible is filled with standard bearers, with shouts to raise high the banner of God. The children of Israel carried standards on their march through the wilderness (see Num. 2). Three Hebrew words describe the standards under which they marched. Each word points to a specific function of the standard or banner. The four primary functions of banners in the Bible are described below:

1. Organization

The tribes of Israel were organized according to God's plan and direction. They did not organize themselves. They never had a committee meeting to develop their organizational bylaws and policies. Instead, the organization of Israel came from the Word of God. The banners He ordained brought order and unity to the camp. They had a purpose, as indicated in Numbers 2:34, "So they camped by their standards, and so they set out, every one by his family, according to his father's household" (NAS).

The standards and banners of the tribes were not for the purpose of taking sides or declaring which tribe or clan was largest or best. Rather, all banners were flown according to God's directive to bring God's people together as a mighty army against their foes.

2. Military

Another type of banner referred to the military function of standards being raised among God's people. The banner was a rallying point for the army. Seeing it flying high lifted the hopes and vision of God's people beyond themselves to the God who would fight and win the battles for them.

At the sound of trumpets, Israel's army would raise the standard of battle and march into combat. Listen to the battle cry in Isaiah:

> Lift ye up a banner upon the high mountain, exalt the voice unto them, shake the hand, that they may go into the gates of the nobles. I have commanded my sanctified ones, I have also called my mighty ones for mine anger, even them that rejoice in my highness. The noise of a multitude in the mountains, like as of a great people; a tumultuous noise of the kingdoms of nations gathered together: the Lord of hosts mustereth the host of the battle (13:2-4).

The Hebrew word for banner, *dagal,* is described as a battle flag in Psalm 20:5: "We will shout for joy when you are victorious and will lift up our *banners* in the name of our God. May the Lord grant all your requests" (NIV, italics added).

3. Spiritual

The Bible also describes standards that God used to

teach spiritual lessons and reveal His truth to His people. In Numbers 21:8-9, God instructed Moses to put a fiery serpent of bronze on a pole to be lifted up before Israel. As they looked upon that standard, they were healed. Jesus refers to the same type of standard in John 3:14-15 when He points to Himself as the standard of salvation, the Savior lifted up on a cross for our salvation and healing.

Prophetically, Isaiah looked ahead to the coming anointed one, the Messiah, as the standard that God would lift before the nations. "In that day the Root of Jesse will stand as a banner for the peoples; the nations will rally to him, and his place of rest will be glorious" (Is. 11:10, NIV).

Of course, that beautiful passage in Song of Solomon 2:4 declares that our loving God is Himself a banner of love over His bride, the church, "He brought me to the banqueting house, and his *banner* over me is love" (italics added).

4. Urgent Proclamation

When an urgent message, proclamation or declaration needed to be made, a standard was raised in a most conspicuous and visible location. Usually, a high elevation was found and the banner or flag was planted there to announce a special occasion or important announcement.

Isaiah 30:17 describes how Israel is to trust the Lord, for under His banner, "A thousand will flee at the threat of one; at the threat of five you will all flee away, till you are left like a *flagstaff* on a mountaintop, like a *banner* on a hill" (NIV, italics added). Banners were used to warn people to flee from the country to the cities for safety (see Jer. 4:6).

Finally, when an army left a banner or standard on a hill unattended, that standard signaled the defeat of that army. "'Their stronghold will fall because of terror; at sight of the battle *standard* their commanders will panic,' declares the Lord, whose fire is in Zion, whose furnace is in Jerusalem" (Is. 31:9, NIV).

Yes, too many in the church have left the banner unattended, and the standard of our God has been left in disrepute because of our sin and rebellion. It's time to declare that Jehovah-Nissi, the Lord Our Banner, reigns.

Standard Bearers Are Birthed at the Altar

I am challenging you right now to build an altar where you live, work or worship. Stop what you are doing. Build an altar. Put on that altar the sin of leaving the banner of God unattended and failing to raise high the standard. Cover yourself and your altar with the banner of His love, crying out for His mercy and forgiveness. Read aloud this verse, "And Moses [put your name in his stead] built an altar, and called the name of it Jehovah-nissi [God is my *Banner*]" (Ex. 17:15).

In the coming chapters I will share with you how to build an altar and how to put yourself on the altar as a living sacrifice so you can become God's standard bearer, raising high His banner (Rom. 12:1). I will share with you how to come out of your desert and into the refreshing rain of God. You will discover how to be a wellspring of living water for your family, church and nation. To build an altar and raise high the standard, you will need to be:

- Repentant.

- Revived and refreshed.

- Restored.

You can't become a standard bearer in the heat of battle. Come out of the desert and into the living waters of God.

Standard bearers never audition for a role or present their past experiences and credentials as if being hired as mercenaries. Standard bearers refuse to drink stagnant waters from old wells. Standard bearers are birthed by the anointing of the Holy Spirit at the altar of Jehovah-nissi.

After the altar there's a time of equipping and preparing, of training and conditioning for the battle. Get ready. Over the hill a battle rages. Around the corner the enemy sets an ambush and lies in wait. Get ready. Don't climb the hill or turn the corner without building an altar and raising high your standard. Don't go blindly into the battle.

Standard bearers are birthed by the anointing of the Holy Spirit at the altar of Jehovah-nissi.

Get under Jehovah-Nissi. You are not the moon or the sun. You have no power on your own. But you can leave the night behind. You can become as fair as the moon and as clear as the sun. You can march in that terrible, awesome army of God, raising high His banner of victory. But a standard bearer's initiation begins at the altar where he is washed in Jesus' blood, cleansed by living water and exposed to His light.

Perhaps you have experienced only religion. Possibly you have lost sight of the standard, the banner of God, amidst a cloak of substitutes. As you stand at the altar of Jehovah God with your hands lifted and your head raised, He will meet you with outstretched arms and once again point you to the blood-stained banner of Jesus Christ.

> *Lord Jesus, create in me an unrelenting, all-consuming desire to the be standard bearer you have called me to be. I repent of wandering in the deserts I have created and drinking from old wells. Flow over me with Your living water. I resolve to pick up the truth of the Word of God which has been so blatantly*

discarded and left at our feet. I stand boldly against the satanic opposition coming against me and my family, and I raise high Your standard and proudly proclaim that You alone are King of kings and Lord of lords. Amen.

Section 1

Become God's
Standard Bearer

Every fresh, new move of God in human history has been preceded by the devotion and righteous passion of one or more individuals who knew their God and knew where they were going. In a day when the foundations of our society are no longer built on the solid rock of Christ but on the sinking sand of worldly relativism, someone must come to the forefront and become what has been lacking in the body of Christ. We need godly, anointed standard bearers to raise high His standard in the church today!

We have not been building on the foundations of faith, hope and love passed down to us from the prophets and the apostles. Instead, we have been building on fear and panic, putting our hope in political masterminds who have manipulated the unthinking, undiscerning masses to perpetuate their own perversions.

While we boast about trivialities as a move of God, a multitude of laity and leaders are still filled with diverse lusts. A flood of moral looseness has so blighted and undermined our homes and our youth that Hollywood's most talented can entice us into sin by taking what is foolish, vile and empty and making it appealing to a deceived generation.

Meanwhile, we the church take unspeakable glory and the manifold cure for all that destroys and so bungle our presentation of the gospel that we appear in the world's eyes to be lying. The world has been lying well while we have been telling the truth badly.

With the foundations eroded, we need standard bearers, not "computer-like" men with memory banks full of dry biblical information. We need warriors who thirst for living waters from the fountain that never runs dry. We need discerning spiritual fathers who lift high the banner of Christ. We need standard bearers who realize that the heart of the human problem is the problem of the human heart and who will take up the standard of the Great Commission to get the life of God back into the hearts of humanity.

Computerized Christianity presents information without love, facts without understanding and knowledge without impartation. It touches the head but misses the heart. It sputters out the dead letter of the law but pours no oil of the Spirit onto a broken heart.

Our man-made approaches for trying to reach our nation have struggled for two generations without producing a move of the Spirit, a genuine culture-shaking revival in which the moral climate of our cities is changed and the nation is impacted with the truth of Almighty God. Our over-organized, streamlined, computerized form of Christianity has been as effective as trying to melt an iceberg with a match.

But there is an answer: God is equipping, preparing and anointing His church to be His standard bearers — a mighty army that is once again laying the foundation of Bible truths. Acts 3:19-21 declares, *"Repent* ye therefore, and be *converted,* that your sins may be blotted out, when the times of *refreshing* shall come from the presence of the Lord; and he shall send Jesus Christ, which before was preached unto you; Whom the heaven must receive until the times of *restitution* of all things, which God hath spoken by the mouth of all his holy prophets since the world began" (italics added).

God is searching for a people, a remnant church, who are repentant, refreshed, restored *and* eagerly expecting the return of Jesus Christ.

God is looking for standard bearers such as:

- Jonathan's armor bearer, to whom Jonathan said,

  Come, and let us go over unto the garrison of these uncircumcised: it may be that the Lord will work for us: for there is no restraint to the Lord to save by many or by few. And his armorbearer said unto him: "Do all that is in thine heart: turn thee; behold, I am with thee according to thy heart" (1 Sam. 14:6-7).

- Elisha, who stayed by Elijah's side and asked of the man of God,

  I pray thee [Elijah], let a double portion of thy spirit be upon me (2 Kin. 2:9).

- Aaron and Hur, who held up Moses' hands during battle so that the enemy could be defeated.

  But Moses' hands were heavy; and they took a

stone, and put it under him, and he sat thereon; and Aaron and Hur stayed up his hands, the one on the one side, and the other on the other side; and his hands were steady until the going down of the sun (Ex. 17:12).

Becoming God's standard bearer begins with:

• Repentance.

Are you willing to change your direction from a guilt-ridden conscience of sin to the liberty and grace of Jesus Christ? Are you willing to turn your back on the dry seasons and walk into God's refreshing rains?

• Revival and refreshing.

Are you willing to receive a fresh baptism of the fire and power of the Holy Spirit and once again feel the winds of revival blowing across your spirit? Are you willing to unstop the well within that is meant to be flowing with living waters?

• Restoration.

Are you ready to have restored to you everything the enemy has stolen and to take back what rightfully belongs to you? Are you willing to dig new wells and receive what God wants to do in your life?

It may seem as though you are caught in an endless cycle, repenting for the same sin night after night as you wet your pillow with tears of remorse.

Possibly you are fed up with trying to live on the emotional charge of weekly church services which leave you powerless to combat the driving forces of darkness during the week.

Your banner may seem full of holes, and from a distance your standard may appear tarnished. Your well may be obstructed so that no water is flowing forth. But let me remind you that you are the head and not the tail (see Deut. 28:13)! You are above and not beneath. You are the victor and not the victim!

Get ready!

I believe that the application of these words — repentance, refreshing and restoration — to your life will bring the breakthrough you have so desperately been seeking and that you will become the mighty standard bearer God has called you to be.

3

Repent to Raise His Standard

In the beginning God existed alone. He searched endlessly throughout eternity for a comrade, a confidante, a companion and a friend among the citizens of heaven. But He found none.

So God created man from the cold, red clay of the earth. For this man, Adam, He built a dwelling named Eden, and there man and God walked as friends. Adam fellowshiped freely with his Father in the brilliance of paradise. Their relationship was one of reckless abandon with no reassurances needed.

With the cool breeze of eternity blowing across his brow, Adam's heart must have been full of confident assurance: *What shall separate me from the love of God* (see Rom. 8:35). But you know the story. Right in the middle of paradise,

Adam — the one purposed to be at God's side as His standard bearer — sided with God's archenemy, committed high treason and led the human family in the greatest rebellion ever known.

The result was sin and death. The image of God was dashed to pieces. Death turned blue the lips of man. Locusts swarmed, devouring the blossom of life and leaving only dust within which man would toil. With a flaming sword, man was banished to the sterile plains outside of Eden and was no longer permitted to walk at God's side.

The knowledge of God was replaced with the knowledge of good and evil. Every atrocity and abomination filled humanity's being. In his better moments, man even tried to substitute doing good for knowing God. Purity of heart which could see God was replaced by a hollowness of heart which pretended to be a god. Out of the darkness of the fall stretched a huge chasm between humanity and God. One single exposure to Satan's corruption carried the communicable disease of sin to man, and it now courses through the veins of every person.

Lawlessness lorded over the land. Man had missed the mark. Sin became the standard while God's standard lay abandoned in a ruined paradise. God hung His head and cried, "It was my friend who forsook me."

I remember the story about the time John Wesley asked his mother the riveting question, "What then is sin?" She replied as a godly mother that sin is anything that impedes the tenderness of your conscience; anything that obscures your sense of God; anything that weakens your reason or dulls your desire for spiritual things or exalts the lordship of your soul and body over that of your spirit. That thing to you is sin.

You may believe that you are God's friend, but the Bible calls you His enemy. "For if, when we were enemies," reads Romans 5:10. What makes you an enemy of God? Sin!

And what is sin? It is missing the mark, God's glory.

Sin is what caused our Kinsman-Redeemer, our High Priest, the Word from before the foundation of the world, to leave His eternal throne and invade earth through a lowly manger. Sin brought Jesus from heaven's majesty to a disgraceful, shameful death on a cross so that He could reconcile, revive, refresh and restore the standard bearer to the Father's side.

But the first message you must hear and the initial call you must obey was first uttered by the Savior and has been echoed by His standard bearers throughout history — "Repent!" Men like John the Baptist, Peter the apostle, St. Augustine, Martin Luther, John Calvin, Jonathan Edwards, John Wesley, George Whitefield, Smith Wigglesworth, Lester Sumrall, Billy Graham and countless others recognized the primary nature of this call.

Without repentance, the next phases — refreshing, revival and restoration — cannot come. The gift of the Holy Spirit cannot come. "*Repent,* and be baptized every one of you in the name of Jesus Christ for the remission of sins, and ye shall receive the gift of the Holy Ghost" (Acts 2:38, italics added).

People vainly seek the presence of God without first repenting and converting. But God hates sin. He demands, "Be holy: for I the Lord your God am holy" (Lev. 19:2). Be certain of this: You cannot know His presence nor His holiness without first turning from your sin and guilt. Repentance was the first adamant message of the early church:

> *Repent* ye therefore, and be converted, that your sins may be blotted out, when the times of refreshing shall come from the presence of the Lord (Acts 3:19, italics added).

The church has no message and no standard to raise

high until she becomes clear as the sun. What does "as clear as the sun" mean? It refers to our response to God. We must forsake, rebuke and reject the shadows of sin threatening to pull us back into the obscure darkness. We must abandon old wells — wells from the world, from past sin, from religious tradition. We will never be the terrible army of banners until we first repent and march out of the night.

> Who is she that looketh forth as the morning, fair as the moon, clear as the sun, and terrible as an army with banners? (Song 6:10).

This text is the foundation for our becoming one of God's standard bearers. Becoming terrible as an army with banners doesn't begin with shouting, praising, dancing, clapping and whirling about. Too often the church has gone rushing into battle with dirty garments and soiled uniforms. Too often the church has tried to call the world to repent before she has left the night of sin, disunity, discord, backbiting, gossip, envy, lust and immorality. We need to come out of our deserts — soiled with past battles and sins — and be washed by living water.

> Let us draw near with a true heart in full assurance of faith, having our hearts sprinkled from an evil conscience, and our bodies washed with pure water (Heb. 10:22).

In Isaiah 58:7 the Spirit of God admonishes us not to "hide ourselves from our own flesh." We have been so busy playing the victim and blaming someone else for our failure to obey the commands of God that we have forgotten we were the ones who made the conscious decision to sin. You may say, "Well, I fell into sin." No, my friend, you dug the pool, built the diving board and plunged headlong into the damning desires and polluted waters hidden within the recesses of your heart.

Before you can progress and rise to the rank of a mighty standard bearer in the kingdom of God you must first hear and respond to His primary call. God's first trumpet call to raise up standard bearers in the church is not to battle but to repentance.

God's first trumpet call to raise up standard bearers in the church is not to battle but to repentance.

Before we can become fair — beautiful, pure and clean — as the moon, we must repent! Before we can become clear — transparent, shining, bright — as the sun, we must repent and convert so that when the refreshing, revival and restoration of God comes, we can receive all God has for us as His standard bearers.

"Repent, for the Kingdom of Heaven Is at Hand"

Jesus will say many things to you in life. He will talk to you of worlds to come and speak of the golden streets of heaven. Jesus will give prophetic unction and fill your ears with divine mysteries. The Word will paint pictures of the galaxies He created and reveal the glory of His majesty. But none of this will He ever speak until His first call and command to you are heard and obeyed, "*Repent;* for the kingdom of heaven is at hand" (Matt. 4:17, italics added).

Don't be sorry when you hear such a call for repentance. Why? For refreshing, revival and restoration always follow repentance.

From what sin do we need to repent? The Holy Spirit woke me from a deep sleep and graphically gave me this definition of sin:

Sin is...
the cut of a knife across a victim's flesh;
the fear in a scream;
the hollowness of an empty stomach;
the snobbery of pride;
the clutch of cancer;
malice in murder;
the clamor of war;
the helplessness of divorce;
epidemic AIDS;
blank stares in the faces of the homeless;
wealth in the pockets of the abortionists;
poverty's despair;
the fear of the past;
the fear of the present;
the fear of the future;
the sob of a child in a bedroom being beaten or
sexually abused by a parent.

Sin is everything cruel, ravaging and painful. It is every blight known to humanity. Sin is dying in a dry season. Sin is trying to drink from polluted wells out of which only polluted waters issue which are filled with disease and death. To satisfy sin's craving people will sell their souls and multitudes will spend eternity in hell. But Jesus' hand reaches across the chasm of sin and stretches forth grace and forgiveness in response to one cosmic act — repentance.

Peter's words to the early church and to us reveal clearly the steps we must take to meet the One who forgives, refreshes and restores. Peter's call to repentance in Acts 3:19-20 states:

- *Repent...* Change your mind, heart, direction and life.

- *Be converted...* Turn *to* God and *away* from sin.

- *That your sins may be blotted out...*

- *When the times of refreshing shall come from the presence of the Lord.*

After repentance we are in a position to receive from the Lord. Living water begins to flow from His Holy Spirit within us.

- *And he shall send Jesus Christ.* Now you are ready to march under the banner of Christ in God's terrible army.

Repentance Isn't a Bypass — It's the Only Throughway

Jesus says, "I am the way" (John 14:6). We cannot bypass sin and expect to get through to God. Jesus is the only throughway to repentance, the only access road. In our ignorance and wickedness we try to bypass the reality of our sin.

We say, "I'm weak."

God says, "You're wicked."

We say, "I'm feeble and sick."

God says, "You're sinful and rebellious."

We say, "I'll straighten myself out."

God says, "You are helplessly and hopelessly lost. Nothing you can do will save you."

Don't try to excuse your sin. Sin is always a deliberate act of your will. You decide to sin. How does it happen? James 1:14-15 describes the destructive path that sin takes in your life.

> But every man is tempted, when he is drawn away of his own lust, and enticed. Then when lust hath conceived, it bringeth forth sin: and sin, when it is finished, bringeth forth death.

Notice the path that leads you into sin and the end result.

- The tool of sin is lust. Your own lusts, desires, wants and cravings grasp for what you should not have or do not need.

- The device of sin is enticement. Sin uses your lust to draw you away from God and toward the world; away from holiness and into all that is profane; away from purity and toward impurity and immorality; away from living water and into the desert; and away from truth into a lie. Like a fish lured by bait or an animal enticed by a trap, you find yourself drawn away from the safety of a loving Father and into the arms of the devourer.

- The effect of sin is death. Lust conceived, bears. Sin gradually and seductively steals from you until you are robbed of life itself.

The Bible says that the "wages of sin is death" (Rom. 6:23). Do you think you are not sinning? Take a step back and look at the death in your life. Ask these questions:

- Are you in a dry season?
- Do you feel parched and empty?
- Is your joy dying?
- Are your relationships dying?
- Is your marriage or family dying?
- Are your plans and hopes dying?
- Is anything or everything that you touch dying?

The only way to turn away from the desert and death is to repent. No, I am not talking about just being sorry or sad about your sin. Sorrow is not repentance. I have seen people fall all over the altar on Sunday consumed with tears and shaking with remorse, only to leave the altar and go about sinning all week. The next Sunday they come to the altar again, crying and expecting to feel something from God.

God's demand on us to become standard bearers requires us to leave the night and look forth to the morning. "Who is she who looketh forth as the morning?" She is a church filled with standard bearers who refuse to return to the night as soon as they leave the church parking lot or the home group or the mission trip. "Fair as the moon and clear as the sun" is not just for the altar or the service or the times with other Christians. Repentance, conversion and becoming fair and clear are not for a moment but for a lifetime.

> ## Sorrow may accompany repentance but sorrow is not repentance.

"Oh, brother," you say, "I backslid last week." Why? "Because the devil made me do it."

No, brother, you did it. Instead of advancing into the morning, you decided to retreat into the night. Give it up! Give up the night. Leave sin behind at the altar once and for all! Get real about repentance.

Sorrow may accompany repentance but sorrow is not repentance.

Repentance is change!

Change your season.

Change your mind.

Change your actions.

Change your direction.

Change your character.

Repentance involves a total change of life.

Jesus came preaching repentance. To the religious He

says repent. In other words change your minds, get a new concept of God's kingdom in your hearts and heads. To those with wealth and power He says repent. Change where you deposit your treasures. Instead of putting treasures where moth and rust corrupt, lay up treasures in heaven (Matt. 6:19-20). Instead of seeking things, seek first God's kingdom and His righteousness (Matt. 6:33).

I knew a man who claimed to be an atheist. He was so crooked he couldn't walk or talk straight. After a few conversations he repented of being an atheist. He changed his mind and handed me a book of Jewish mysticism and reincarnation and said, "Read it." Oh, he believed he had repented and turned, but he had turned the wrong way!

Without Christ, you can repent of one evil thing and be caught in the snares of another. Don't forsake one dry well for another. Being sorry and turning away from one sin isn't enough. You must turn to Christ.

Pay close attention here. You can be truly sorry and filled with sorrow for your sin and not be repentant. God isn't interested in your apology. He wants you to change — your mind, heart, actions and life and turn toward Him.

Repentance — A New Direction for Your Life

When you repent, you change directions. A standard bearer must go the same direction as his Master. You are going your own direction before you repent. The Bible says, "There is a way that seemeth right unto a man, but the end thereof are the ways of death" (Prov. 16:25).

Before you became a Christian you were headed toward hell. But then you repented and changed directions. Now where are you headed? Your new direction is the kingdom of God. Before you repented, you lived in the night and dwelt in the shadows; you wandered aimlessly in the desert. Now you look forth as the morning. Now you dispel the shadows, becoming fair as the moon and clear as the sun. Now you march forward into the kingdom of God as a terrible army with banners, possessing the land where you live and taking back the territory the enemy has stolen. You are digging new wells and plummeting deep into the aquifers of God.

"Repent, for the kingdom of God is at hand" (Matt. 4:17). Every kingdom must have a king. In sin, your king was Satan, and your domain was darkness. In God's kingdom, He alone is king. To be king means to be sovereign. Sovereignty implies authority, power and rule. God rules. We do not.

In the kingdom of heaven you don't presume to tell God anything. You simply bow your head in reverence to the King of kings. No longer do you pray for what *you* want. Rather, the kingdom prayer is: "*Thy* kingdom come. *Thy* will be done, in earth as it is in heaven" (Matt. 6:10, italics added).

Jesus established the heavenly order on earth. God's kingdom is His right to govern every minute molecule of human existence. God's kingdom is His right of lordship, authority, power and law. God declares who shall be exalted and who shall be brought low. He shows mercy to whom He decides to show mercy. His say is final and absolute in our lives, marriages, families, vocations and church. He is King and we are not! Here is my "deep revelation:" He is God and you are not!

God will not share His throne with anyone or anything else. The ancient Israelites tried to make God just a *part* of their lives. They desired to worship God, but also worship Baal and Molech. But God is a jealous God. We are to have no other gods before Him (Ex. 20:3).

Like ancient Israel, we bring our sacrifices and cry before God, trying to atone for our sin. But we do not repent of our materialism, immorality, idolatry or lusts. We try to serve both God and man. We try to drink from many wells instead of the one true well of God. God hates crying at the altar when there is no repentance.

> I hate, I despise your feast days, and I will not smell in your solemn assemblies. Though ye offer me burnt offerings and your meat offerings, I will not accept them: neither will I regard the peace offerings of your fat beasts. Take thou away from me the noise of thy songs; for I will not hear the melody of thy viols. But let judgment run down as waters, and righteousness as a mighty stream (Amos 5:21-24).

Let the streams and waters of God loose in your life through repentance.

The kingdom of heaven comes to us now. Before we repent, His kingdom is not within us. Rather, His kingdom is among us, in our midst. With repentance, the kingdom moves from without to within us (Luke 17:21). New Age false prophets deceive the lost by telling them that something of God is within each person and that each of us must discover the god within. Believe me, the god within is an idol. "The heart is deceitful and desperately wicked, who can know it?" (Jer. 17:9). God's kingdom confronts us from without demanding repentance so that the King of glory might come in and reign in our lives forever.

Don't come dancing and singing to the altar without repentance. Don't weep and wail before God without repentance. Don't promise to leave sin behind at church when you return to live in sin at home.

God warns us: "Go ahead. Have your day. Have your feast. Sing your song. Dance your dance. Laugh your laugh. Cry your tears. Shout your shouts. Roll or fall down. But without repentance, I will not be there."

We expect to make our plans and then have God bless them. We expect to include God in our activities instead of abandoning our activities to seek His face. Forget your goals and objectives. Leave behind your schemes and devices. Separate yourself from the ways of the world. Repent!

God warns us: "Without repentance, I will not be there."

Slam your door. Lock your lock. Fall on your face. Humble yourself. Find out God's plan. Hear His voice. Change from your ways to His way. Leave your old wells. Repent! The demand is immediate. Don't wait for the kingdom of God to come. It is here. It is time to enthrone the exiled King, kiss His scepter, bow your knee and say, "Lead on, O King eternal."

Repent — Put on Sackcloth

Remember Jonah's fiery preaching about repentance to the city of Nineveh? How did the mightiest man in the city respond? What did the king of Nineveh do when called to repentance?

> For word came unto the king of Nineveh, and he arose from his throne, and he laid his robe from him, and covered him with sackcloth, and sat in ashes (Jon. 3:6).

Jonah never wanted to go to the enemies of Israel, the Assyrians, and preach the message of repentance. He ran the other direction. But God sent a storm and a rescue squad in the belly of a fish to bring Jonah back to Nineveh. With Jonah's message came revival, refreshing and restoration to a city. But first, there had to be repentance.

The king and the people repented, "So the people of Nineveh believed God, and proclaimed a fast, and put on sackcloth, from the greatest of them even to the least of them" (Jon. 3:5).

Second Chronicles 7:14 sounds the trumpet call to any person who would become a standard bearer for the King:

> If my people, who are called by my name, shall humble themselves, and pray, and seek my face, and turn from their wicked ways; then will I hear from heaven, and will forgive their sin, and will heal their land.

To march in His army, to raise His standard, we must first humble ourselves, pray, seek God's face and *turn from our wicked ways*. That's repentance. Only after repentance does God hear from heaven, forgive us and heal our land.

It's time to put on sackcloth, sit in the ashes of repentance and cry out to God for His forgiving mercy in Christ Jesus. Perhaps you have read these words but believe yourself to be exempt from Jesus' call of repentance. You may think you are living a good life and are free from sin. But the convicting words of God confront you: "If we say that we have no sin, we deceive ourselves, and the truth is not in us" (1 John 1:8).

The truth steps on our toes, shouts in our faces and spotlights the darkness in our hearts that is filled with cesspools of unrighteousness. "*All* have sinned and fallen short of the glory of God!" (Rom. 3:23, italics added, NIV).

The first step toward becoming God's standard bearer is repentance — putting on sackcloth and rending our hearts before God. Acts 2:38 and 3:19 both begin with the same demand: *Repent!* Of what do you need to repent?

1. Sins of commission.

These are sins that you know full well not to commit and you do them anyway. You have asked God over and over to forgive you of these sins, but they plague and haunt your life. Such sins seem to follow you wherever you go. About the time that you claim victory over them, you sin again, doing what you know not to do.

Paul says, "But the evil which I would not, that I do" (Rom. 7:19b). Do you ever find yourself repeatedly doing what you know to be wrong? Sin is the deadliest addiction. Our first response to addictive sin might be to deny it. Don't deny it! Confess and repent of your sins of commission.

2. Sins of omission.

These are things you fail to do that you know you should do. We should pray, but we are mired in the sin of prayerlessness. We should worship, but we find ourselves distracted by everything under the sun while lifting our hands to heaven. We should love and pray for our enemies, but we do not.

There are words God has given you to say, but you refuse to speak them because of your fear of what man will think. There are places God has sent you to witness and mighty acts of service and ministry He has commissioned you to do, but you refrain from going and doing them because of shame and fear. Paul writes, "The good that I would I do not" (Rom. 7:19).

We need to repent of both sins of commission and sins of omission. God is holding us accountable for doing the things we shouldn't do, and for not doing the things we should. Now is the time to repent. Are you ready?

Are you ready to stop doing that thing you know not to do? God can deliver you from the addiction of sin.

Are you ready to do what you know is right? God can empower you to walk in righteousness.

Are you ready to change your mind? If so, God can renew your mind.

Are you ready to turn from sin and wickedness? If so, God can forgive you.

Are you ready to admit your helplessness and hopelessness? If so, God can restore you.

Are you ready for the dry season to end? If so, Christ will bring forth living water from your life.

Are you ready to enthrone the exiled King? If so, Christ will establish His throne on the seat of your heart.

Are you ready to ascribe to His lordship? If so, Christ will be Lord over all your life.

Hear the promise of God. "If we confess our sins, he is faithful and just to forgive us our sins, and to cleanse us from all unrighteousness" (1 John 1:9). Remember, it is the goodness of God which leads you to repentance (Rom. 2:4). God stands with open arms to offer you a glorious banquet in place of the husks of this world which you have been consuming. The convicting power of the Holy Spirit is to the spirit what pain is to the body — it is not the problem but only an indication that one exists.

Before you stand in the courts of praise, you must first sit in the sackcloth and ashes of repentance. Before you enter into the refreshing presence of the Lord, you must first repent of sin and convert, turning completely toward the Lord. To become clear as the sun, you must first leave the night, the shadows and the darkness behind you once and for all. Only when you are washed in the blood of the Lamb will you know the cleansing from sin that brings life out of death and resurrection out of the grave of the past.

Are you ready for revival, refreshing and restoration as a standard bearer to the King of kings and Lord of lords? Then pray:

> *Father, reveal unto me the hidden sin of my heart. Deliver me from the sins of omission and commission which have so plagued my*

life. I have walked the floor and wept over my sins but have not changed. But right now I make a conscious decision to change my mind about You and turn toward Your kingdom. I forsake the desert. I rebuke the dry season. I lay my sin at the altar of my heart. I declare Your sovereignty in my life and pick up the standard, saying, "Lead on, O King eternal!"

CHAPTER 4

Revived and Refreshed

In a time when a powerless Pentecost has been the norm rather than the exception, with more deserts than downpours, more perversion than power, more playboys than prophets, more compromise than conviction, we need the One who condescends to indwell mortals and to fill us full of Himself. But let us first count the cost.

Though Pentecost meant power to the disciples, it also meant prison and banishment from organized religion. Though Pentecost brought favor from God, it also brought hatred from men. Though Pentecost produced great miracles, it also produced mighty obstacles. Pentecost required men to leave the old wells of past tradition and drink from the fresh outpourings of the Holy Spirit.

Why do we hang a sign outside our church to announce

that we are Pentecostal? Because without the sign no one could identify us. Most of the time, the sign outside the church is the only sign anyone will see. Why? When they get inside, they find nothing more than placating pastors afraid to speak in tongues or allow the other gifts of the Holy Spirit to be manifested lest they offend someone of influence in their congregation. Yes, even those who claim to be "Spirit-filled" have allowed their waters to become stagnant and their oases to return to desert dunes.

Drive through a town after a tornado has ravaged its buildings. You do not have to be told that a mighty wind has passed through the place, nor do you need an explanation of other natural displays of God's power. A fire is self-announcing. A flood leaves unmistakable evidence of its presence. Pentecost is to be the evidence of the wind, fire and power of the Holy Spirit, yet it is not apparent in our churches and in our lives. Because we no longer pray in tongues in private, we have no power in public. Our being devoid of heaven's language makes us void of an earthly word. We preach in our best-pressed suits, but we fail to pierce the heavenlies with our prayers.

We have a shout in the sanctuary but no clout in the Spirit. We claim authority, but we don't gain any meaningful ground. We write songs about victory over evil that are more suitable for the playground than for the battleground. We have become proficient in the dialect of men and unversed in the voice of heaven!

Many who claim they have experienced the baptism of the Holy Spirit are more dead than alive, more off than on, more wrong than right. Some are more spirit-frilled than Spirit-filled. We have become satisfied with quick showers instead of desiring deluges from the floodgates of heaven. We have grown accustomed to the "outer fringe of God's works and have forgotten the reality of His power."

Whenever evil mires the work of God, our flesh reasserts

itself and our lack of fruit condemns the prayerless, powerless and passionless religion we masquerade as Christianity. We need another drenching downpour of Pentecostal power.

Standard bearers who have truly repented before God are ready to exchange:

- Their dignity for a demonstration.

- Their degrees for a revelation.

- Their marketing for miracles.

- Their reputation for repentance.

- Their tongues of poison for tongues of fire set ablaze by the Holy Spirit of God.

It's time to raise the standard in the church again. It's time for the church to launch out into the proverbial deep waters where we cannot stand by our own strength and efforts and where we must be sustained by the river and wind of the Holy Spirit that fills us to overflowing with God's power and strength.

Once we repent of our mediocrity, our sin and our efforts to be normal, and once we start desiring the refreshing of God, we will see God's wind begin to fill our sails. In Acts 3:19, we see that after repentance and conversion come the times of refreshing in God's presence.

I want you to know that God is in the refreshing business. God is in the restoration business. God is going to lean over the pavilions of glory and the sapphire sill of heaven's gate. He is going to draw in a breath of eternal air and begin to blow a blast, a whirlwind from heaven that will refresh all of His people. A wind is starting to blow in the church. The sounds of wind and rain, of God's refreshing, are moving the church beyond the status quo which we have known for so long. God is ready to refresh and revive your life.

She Is a Revived, Refreshed church

Remember our text in Song of Solomon 6:10, "Who is she that looketh forth as the morning, fair as the moon, clear as the sun, and terrible as an army with banners"? She is not just an ordinary church. She is a church being blown by the wind of God. She is a revived, refreshed church marked by moral integrity, physical purity, spiritual intensity, personal devotion and holiness unto the Lord. She lives for His righteousness' sake and raises high His standard.

A church filled with repentant standard bearers is no longer content with empty pews or, worse yet, pew-sitters. She is a church breaking forth as the morning. Isaiah 60:1 describes such a church, "Arise, shine; for thy light is come, and the glory of the Lord is risen upon thee."

A church that looketh forth as the morning lives in the spiritual atmosphere of expectancy with a leadership who refuses to move until God moves and refuses to give up until God gives all of Himself to them.

What about the priests, the preachers, the leaders of such a revived church? What are they like? Joel gives this description:

> Gird yourselves, and lament, ye priests: howl [wail], ye ministers of the altar: come, lie all night in sackcloth, ye ministers of my God: for the meat offering and the drink offering is withholden from the house of your God (Joel 1:13).

What kind of pastoral leadership do we need in the revived and refreshed church of God's people? We need leaders who are willing to stay up all night in sackcloth seeking God and crying out for more of Him and less of them. We need leaders more concerned for the lost than for how the world views them. We need priests so thirsty for a drink of living water from the river of God that they will pray the floodgates of heaven open. We need priests who have totally left the night behind and are willing to look forth into the morning.

God says to His priests that He desires a rending of hearts, not garments.

> Rend your heart, and not your garments, and turn unto the Lord your God: for he is gracious and merciful, slow to anger, and of great kindness, and repenteth him of the evil (Joel 2:13).

God desires to send both the former and the latter rain (Hos. 6:3). He wants to send both the harvest and the planting rain in the same month. The sowing and the reaping will be coming at the same time.

We are looking for a harvest in which the reapers overtake the sowers; for a time when before your mind can send the message to speak His name, He will be found with you (Is. 37:30; Amos 9:13). Do you know what that means? There will be no dry season but a perpetual flood of God's provision in every area of your life!

God says to His priests that He desires a rending of hearts, not garments.

What does it mean for leaders? They must raise up standard bearers, workers in the harvest, to work and witness day and night.

But first it is the commandment of God for His standard bearers to be *filled* with the Holy Spirit. They must be empowered to do what they are called to do.

In Exodus, Bezaleel was filled with the Spirit of God,

empowering him to build the tabernacle. John the Baptist was filled from his mother's womb, preparing him for effective ministry. On the day of Pentecost, Peter was filled with the Holy Spirit, allowing him to preach with resurrection power.

Being filled with the Holy Spirit means literally to be "propelled forward" as a sail is filled with the wind (Eph. 5:18).

Some say that the revival will never happen, the wind of God will never blow, and the rain will never come. Like the wicked generation of Noah's day and the religious hypocrites of Jesus' day, they fail to recognize the move of God and may miss their day of visitation (Is. 10:3; Hos. 9:7).

God declares that in the last days He will pour out His Spirit on all flesh (Acts 2:17). Those standard bearers ready for the harvest will experience the revival and the refreshing. Like parched land drinking in the sudden rain, those thirsting and hungering for righteousness will be filled. Before the rain, the wind begins to blow, letting us know that a refreshing is about to be poured out.

Get Ready: The Wind Is About to Blow

Prepare for the wind to blow in your life. Watch out! I'm not talking about a gentle breeze to refresh you. God is a whirlwind, a mighty tornado of eternal proportions, and He is ready to release His life into you as He did into Job, "Then the Lord answered Job out of the whirlwind" (Job 38:1).

God always distinguishes Himself by a wind. In the wind God sends propulsion and provision. Remember how God propelled the Red Sea with a strong east wind so that dry ground appeared? Remember how God provided the wind as a deliverance to the children of Israel, allowing them to cross the Red Sea and escape the pursuing armies of Pharaoh (Ex. 14:21)? Remember how God passed by Elijah with a great and strong wind (1 Kin. 19:11)?

From the very beginning, God's wind and breath have been a propulsion and provision for us. God breathed the wind of His breath into us and we became living souls (Gen. 2:7). We were propelled from clay into living bodies and provided with His breath so that life might be sustained in our earthen vessels.

God's wind of refreshing needs to blow in your life. His wind sweeps away all ritualism, legalism, religious performance and vain attempts to please man. His wind brings genuine Pentecostal power.

There they gathered in an upper room, 120 faithful followers waiting for God's wind. There were no human props, no illustrated sermons, no special music, no finely tuned sound system, no church building funds and no monuments or shrines. With no human effort or planning, the wind of God began to blow, "And suddenly there came a sound from heaven as of a rushing mighty wind, and it filled all the house where they were sitting" (Acts 2:2). A divine "*Go*" from the wind of God entered their souls.

We have trusted too much in organizations, plans, goals, objectives and schedules. We have organized too much with our flowcharts and into our committees and departments. Let His wind clear it all away. God will blow across all human barriers — political, educational, social, racial, religious and financial. With all barriers blown down, she, the church, will come forth into the morning as a mighty, terrible army under the banner of Christ as one people, one body, serving Christ in one accord.

God's wind will blow your pride and pretensions away. His wind, to say the least, will disrupt your plans.

We've come to expect the wind of Pentecost to blow breezily through our lives without ruffling our dainty clothes, our carefully prepared orders of service and our structures of ministry. I'm not talking about this kind of pleasant push from the Holy Spirit. I'm telling you, the whirlwind is coming!

We've come to expect the wind of Pentecost to blow breezily through our lives without ruffling our dainty clothes, our carefully prepared orders of service and our structures of ministry.

I am seeing a genuine refreshing raising up standard bearers throughout the church who are filled with resurrection power. It is bigger than I am, bigger than a television ministry, bigger than a denomination and bigger than any revelation we can envision. I'm talking about a revival so big that a stadium cannot contain it — one that can't be penciled in and organized to fit between the lines of your day planner or calendar. This revival is so immense that only heaven can develop it.

God's Word promises the refreshing. "Times of refreshing shall come from the presence of the Lord" (Acts 3:19). After repenting and converting, we no longer live in the "ifs" of refreshing. Stop saying, "*If* God refreshes us. *If* God revives us." He has spoken it, and it is done. He *is* refreshing and reviving. Listen to what God says,

> Remember ye not the former things, neither consider the things of old. Behold, I will do a new thing; now it shall spring forth; shall ye not know it? I will even make a way in the wilderness, and rivers in the desert (Is. 43:18-19).

The way is made, and the rivers are flowing. Get ready! They are coming upon you now.

Don't Be Discouraged — The Rain Is Coming

God, send the rain! The Old Testament prophets saw the rain coming. Like the dark wall of pouring rain sweeping in from the horizon across a Kansas wheat field, the approaching rain of Pentecost could be seen for centuries by the prophets. Isaiah knew we would speak with tongues. Zechariah said, "It is going to fall like rain!" (10:1). Amos warned, "It will take some preparation." Hosea revealed, "It will take the breaking up of fallow ground!" (10:12). And after the rain began falling at Pentecost, Peter said that angels desired to look upon it.

The rain may be falling all around us, yet we find ourselves personally in a drought.

When my sister and I were children, we lived on the south end of Columbus, Ohio. Spring rains would fall, and we would be out in the front yard whirling, dancing and enjoying the rain. Then we would run through the house out into the backyard, but the strangest thing happened. The rain stopped, or so it seemed. It was raining in the front yard but not in the back. Have you ever seen it pouring rain on one side of town and dry as a bone on the other? It's happening in the church right now. Some standard bearers are in a downpour while others are still waiting for the refreshing revival of God.

Why is that? Do you have your sails in the wrong position? Are you facing man and not God? Are you being blown by the dry winds of this world instead of receiving the rushing wind of fire? Adjust your sails. Catch the wind.

But you may be on the wrong side of the wind. Don't expect to catch the wind where you caught it before. God says to you as He said to the Israelites, "For the land, whither thou goest in to possess it, is not as the land of Egypt, from whence ye came out...But the land, whether ye go to possess it, is a land of hills and valleys, and drinketh water of the rain of heaven" (Deut. 11:10-11).

God was preparing His people for the land of hills and valleys, ups and downs. He was in charge. God had delivered them from Egyptian slavery, pagan religion and bondage. The past was finished. Newness was coming.

Now God is preparing you so get ready. You can walk in the rain. You can drink from an ever-flowing well. You can leave the desert and the dry season. You can catch the wind of God. You are His standard bearer. The past is forgiven, and the chains of bondage are broken.

At times the drought seems like it will never end. It appears that the night will last forever. Look forth, the morning is coming and you will be fair as the moon and as clear as the sun. I know you don't feel like a terrible army with banners now, but feelings are not reality. The truth you stand on is not your feelings, not what the preacher preaches, not what any creed claims. Your truth is God's Word. He says that you will look forth as the morning and march terrible as an army with banners (Song 6:10).

You have prayed until your tongue is swollen and completely dry. You have confessed every confession book until the pages are worn, torn and falling out. The dry heat of battle brings sweat to your brow. You throw your spiritual windows open hoping to feel a little breeze and to see a small cloud on the horizon foretelling a coming rain. God demands of you the patience spoken of in James:

> Elias was a man subject to like passions as we are, and he prayed earnestly that it might not rain: and it rained not on the earth by the space of three years and six months. And he prayed again, and the heaven gave rain, and the earth brought forth her fruit (5:17-18).

Listen! The standard bearers being raised up in these last days will not stand still at midnight. We will refuse to give up in the night. Boldly confessing that joy comes in the morning, we will rebuke darkness. We are not those who go into the night never to come out again. We turn our backs on the desert shouting, "No dry season." Like Caleb and Joshua, we do not faint at the sight of giants. We know that the promised land — not the wilderness — is our destiny.

We are not those who enter the fiery furnace to perish there. Yes, we pass through the deep water, but we do not drown. Morning is coming, declares Isaiah. She, the church — that's us — is going forth as the morning.

You need to get ready to walk out of the darkness. You need to get ready to march out of the valley. Hoist your sails and be filled with the Holy Spirit, the mighty wind of God.

The atmosphere of refreshing is one of expectancy, and that's the breeding ground for miracles. It doesn't matter what you are going through.

> Like Caleb and Joshua, we do not faint at the sight of giants. We know that the promised land — not the wilderness — is our destiny.

It doesn't matter how dark your circumstances are or how deep the waters are which you feel are about to drown you. You are going to make it all the way to the other side. Remember God's promise, "When thou passest through the waters, I will be with thee; and through the rivers, they shall not overflow thee" (Is. 43:2). You will make it to the other side. God didn't bring you this far to let you down. He didn't teach you to swim to let you drown. He will see you through to the times of refreshing.

God, Send Revival Fire

John the Baptist prophetically preached about the fire that fell in Acts 2. He proclaimed,

> I indeed baptize you with water unto repentance: but he that cometh after me is mightier than I, whose shoes I am not worthy to bear: he shall baptize you with the Holy Ghost, and with fire (Matt. 3:11).

John's prophetic statement doesn't end with the baptism of fire. He also speaks of a purging, devouring, cleansing and unquenchable fire that comes through Christ. He says, "Whose fan is in his hand, and he will thoroughly purge his floor, and gather his wheat into the garner; but he will burn up the chaff with unquenchable fire" (Matt. 3:12).

An Old Testament parallel or counterpart to this text speaks of the fire that devours and purges. Isaiah 33:10-12 reveals,

> Now will I rise, saith the Lord; now will I be exalted; now will I lift up myself. Ye shall conceive chaff, ye shall bring forth stubble: your breath, as fire, shall devour you. And the people shall be as the burnings of lime: as thorns cut up shall they be burned in the fire.

When the fire of revival falls upon the church, God's fire burns, purges and cleanses sinners in the camp.

Yes, there are sinners in the church. Isaiah 33:14 declares, "The sinners in Zion are afraid." Some stand in dire need of repentance. Jeremiah observed that God's people had become so indifferent to sin that they couldn't even blush at the sight of their shame (Jer. 6:15). That is happening in the church today. How we need God's fire in the church! The revival fire that sweeps through the church will be twofold: a devouring fire and an everlasting, baptizing fire.

God's judgment against Judah's enemy Assyria was like a devouring fire.

> Behold, the name of the Lord cometh from far, burning with his anger, and the burden thereof is heavy: his lips are full of indignation, and his tongue as a *devouring fire*...And the Lord shall cause his glorious voice to be heard, and shall show the lighting down of his arm, with the indignation of his anger, and with the flame of a *devouring fire,* with scattering, and tempest, and hailstones (Is. 30:27,30, italics added).

When the armies of Assyria besieged Jerusalem, those within the walls of the city were afraid. All they could do was watch the adversary pound against the gates. In a sense, they knew nothing of the purging fire of God. They simply wanted "to hold down the fort."

Many in the church today still sit inside the walls fearing the enemy, holding the fort and hoping that the devil cannot break in. Just as there were sinners in Zion, ancient Israel, there are sinners in today's Zion, the church. Yes, the unregenerate need to know about the judging fire of God, but so do the backsliders, the criticizers, the gossipers and the backbiters. There are sinners in the camp.

Not only did the enemy Assyrians experience the terrifying fire of God, but those behind the walls also witnessed it and trembled. We need a devouring fire from God to burn up the chaff and cleanse away our sin. Jesus came bringing a devouring fire to cleanse God's people.

We must consider two kinds of fires in revival. John said that Jesus would baptize with fire and that He would burn the chaff with unquenchable fire. In fact, the same fire of God does both. His devouring fire burns away all sin, unholiness and impurity, while His baptizing fire fills us with power, boldness and the Holy Spirit.

Listen to the questions asked in Isaiah 33:14. "Who among us shall dwell with the devouring fire? who among us shall dwell with everlasting burnings?" Let me ask a few questions that are raised in my spirit by this text.

1. Who can merely visit this kind of fire?

Weekend warriors cannot show up at church only on Sunday and expect to dwell in the fire. If it doesn't burn in your bones, you will lose the fire during the week and be consumed by the fire on the weekend.

2. Who can flee this kind of fire?

There is no place to run in revival. All sin is exposed. You can't run from the convicting fire of the Holy Spirit when the fire comes. We tend to rebuke the devil. No, my friend, the fire doesn't come from the enemy. God is in the fire. He is trying to work His purpose in you. He is purging the dross out of your life. No, you cannot visit the fire nor can you run from it.

3. Who can fight this fire?

Why do you resist the work of God? Why do you try to disobey the voice of God in your life?

If you want revival and refreshing, you must be prepared for the fire. Ananias and Sapphira were drawn to the baptizing fire but lacked the fear of God needed for His devouring fire. They fought the fire. They wanted the blessing but thought that they could lie to the Holy Spirit. Both were destroyed by God's fire. The chaff was burned, and they lost their lives (see Acts 5:1-10).

Yes, God's revival fire will burn and baptize. It will burn the chaff right out of you, your household, your family, your workplace and your church. We pray for the fire as ancient Israel did, hoping that only our enemies and not ourselves will be burnt with unquenchable fire. Believe me, all of us need that purging fire which prepares us to receive the eternal fire we want to burn in our spirits. The same fire that baptizes also burns, purges, cleanses and prepares us to live a holy life.

We are to burn as clear as the sun. Fire is heat, light and passion. Jesus said that He is the light of the world. That's fire! Jesus also embodied the love of the Father. That's passion. The baptizing fire and passion burning within Jesus explodes in our midst as a consuming fire. God in our midst is "a consuming fire" (Heb. 12:29).

Fire is the presence of God. His presence comes to devour and to baptize, to cleanse us from sin and to fill us with the everlasting fire of the Holy Spirit. Fire burns what is not holy into nothing. Fire refines gold. Fire strengthens steel. The dross gets destroyed, and the impurities are burnt away. But what remains is hard, strong, pure and holy.

If the church is to raise up anointed standard bearers who are as clear as the sun and who carry the banner of Christ, then we need God's fire, both purging and baptizing. So we cry, "God, revive your church as she looketh forth in the morning, fair as the moon and clear as the sun. God, revive your church by sending your devouring and baptizing fire!"

4. Who can live in the fire?

Isaiah answers our question. "He that walketh righteously, and speaketh uprightly; he that despiseth the gain of oppressions, that shaketh his hands from holding of bribes, that stoppeth his ears from hearing of blood, and shutteth his eyes from seeing evil; He shall dwell on high: his place of defence shall be the munitions of rocks: bread shall be given him; his waters shall be sure" (Is. 33:15-16).

Once purged and baptized by fire, what is the anointed standard bearer of Jesus Christ like? He walks in righteousness. He speaks truth. He hates injustice. He keeps evil from his ears and eyes. He dwells in God's presence knowing that the source for all his physical and spiritual needs is God and God alone.

That terrible army marching under the banner of Christ welcomes the purging, devouring fire of the Holy Spirit for purification and the baptizing fire for power to go boldly into the world. God, send the fire! With the wind, rain and fire of God comes His power! His refreshing fills us with power!

With Refreshing Comes God's Power

Power is the peculiar prerogative of God alone. All true and lasting power resides in Him. One Greek word for power is *dunamis* from which we get the English word *dynamite*. Within that one word resides the meanings of miracle-working power, authoritative power and awesome, mighty power. All power belongs to God, "God hath spoken once; twice have I heard this that power belongeth unto God" (Ps. 62:11).

God's power both resides and is manifested in the trinity. God's creative power brought the heavens and the earth into being. Without the Son, who is the Word of God, "was not anything made that was made" (John 1:3). By Him all things consist and hold together" (Col. 1:17). Through the Holy Spirit, God's power is manifested in miracles, signs, wonders and gifts.

The refreshing of God will be marked by His power. The same power which created the universe and conceived the Savior will reside in us, bringing resurrection power into our daily lives. "And what is the exceeding greatness of his power to us-ward who believe, according to the working of his mighty power, which he wrought in Christ, when he raised him from the dead, and set him at his own right hand in the heavenly places" (Eph. 1:19-20).

Are you ready for the refreshing, for the revival, resurrection power that will come into your life after repentance and conversion? Hear the promise of God: "But ye shall receive power, after that the Holy Ghost is come upon you" (Acts 1:8).

God's power makes His church a terrible army going forth under the banner of Christ. His power works miracles, opens blind eyes, sets free the captives, heals the sick and delivers from every bondage. The power of God defeats Satan at every turn, putting him where he belongs — under our feet. Get ready for the miracle-working power of God that comes in times of refreshing. His power will come suddenly today just as in the days of the apostles.

Suddenly...the Refreshing Comes

Malachi declared that revival would come suddenly. "Behold, I [God] will send my messenger, and he shall prepare the way before me: and the Lord, whom ye seek, shall *suddenly* come to his temple, even the messenger of the covenant, whom ye delight in: behold, he shall come, saith the Lord of hosts" (Mal. 3:1, italics added).

This revival and refreshing will send standard bearers to harvest where they did not reap, and they will overtake the sowers sowing their seed. This is a sudden refreshing. Can you see God's vision for you?

- You will sense a dry season trying to surround you, and suddenly God's rain will come.

- You may have a tumor or other illness in your body,

85

and suddenly it will be gone.

- Your church will be half empty, and suddenly people will be standing in line trying to get in.

- Your children may be rebellious and disrespectful, and suddenly they will be saved and reconciled to God and to you.

- Your spouse may leave home, but suddenly he or she will fall under conviction, repent and be restored to you.

- Your finances may be stretched and falling apart, and suddenly you will be able to give to God's work out of your abundance, not out of your lack.

Suddenly, God's revival and refreshing will overtake you. Are you ready?

Can you imagine it? The early church who was caught up in the winds of Pentecost with only 120 members didn't have a marketing team. No advertisements appeared on television. No ads were in the newspaper. No radio beamed their message to walkmans tuned in to the news. There were no book tables, tape offers, mailing lists, faxes or Web pages on the Internet to get out the message. The gospel was manifested in outward, visible displays, inward spiritual power and mighty signs and wonders of the Holy Spirit to the uttermost parts of the earth.

That first revival didn't need electric power or nuclear power. Pentecost didn't depend on political power or financial power. Neither Wall Street nor Madison Avenue nor Main Street were involved. The Holy Spirit wind had its own power — God's power. "But ye shall receive power, after that the Holy Ghost is come upon you: and ye shall be witnesses unto me" (Acts 1:8).

God's first-century standard bearers didn't carry heavy baggage, cumbersome creeds or sophisticated structures.

They simply let the wind, fire and power of the Holy Spirit propel them. And propel them it did — across the hills of Judea and Samaria, through the hills of Rome and the deserts of Africa, across the plains of Persia to the outer regions of the earth. What was the result? The world was turned upside down (Acts 17:6).

So when the Holy Spirit blows, hoist your sails. When His fire falls, open wide your spirit and allow Him to purge and baptize you. When His power comes, let Him infuse you with authority to overcome depravity, disease, deception, defeat and the devil. Let your life be filled with His purpose. Trade your mechanical irrigation for divine intervention.

As Jesus hung on the cross dying for our sins, the wind of God swept over the land, ran through the temple and ripped in two the veil covering the holy of holies. In the same way, allow His Spirit to explode into your life and refresh you with His wind, rain, fire and power. Pray:

> *Lord, I have been trying to be a standard bearer on my own. But now I am ready to encounter Your wind. I am ready to let You refresh me with the rain of Your Spirit. I am ready to experience Your fire. I am ready to be infused once again with Your power. Fill me with fresh anointing, fresh hope and fresh vision. Let there be more of You and less of me. Every hindrance that the devil has erected against me is blown away at this moment because what is happening in me is greater than what is happening to me. I exclaim, "I am a Holy-Spirit-filled, refreshed standard bearer and a terror to my enemies!" Amen.*

5

Restored for Jesus' Return

My pastor, Dr. Lester Sumrall, found himself some fifty years ago in the middle of a Central American rain forest. Going about his ministry he came across a witch doctor. The witch doctor held a bullfrog, a symbol of satanic power. He poured a mixture of human blood and alcohol into the mouth of the bullfrog and then danced around it making satanic incantations. Next, he opened the mouth of the frog and drank the mixture of human blood and alcohol in worship to demonic spirits.

Fortunately, my pastor had not been raised in the School of Secular Humanistic, People-pleasing, Pablum-pumping Preachers. Brother Sumrall did not tell the witch doctor that they were having a revival meeting at their church that week and that it would be good if he could drop by. Nor did he tell him to make an appointment with a staff psychiatrist and walk through a twelve-step deliverance program. Dr. Sumrall simply slapped his hands on the side of the man's head and said, "Come out!"

The man fell over with a thud, got back up born again and began speaking in the heavenly language of the Holy Spirit. Dr. Sumrall then went back to the place where he was staying. They didn't have the Hilton or Hyatt at that time. He stayed in the homes of the hosts of the meeting. There was no air conditioning in his small room which had a simple bed up against the wall. Dr. Sumrall laid down in his bed and began to fall asleep.

The window was open, and the curtains were blowing in the hot, summer's night breeze. Suddenly, the sultry heat of the night disappeared and a damp, cold chill filled the room. He began to shiver and shake as an ominous wind blew through the room and stood the curtains straight out from the window.

Dr. Sumrall's bed began to shake so violently that it rocked across the room and out into the middle of the floor.

"I've had about enough of this," Dr. Sumrall said. He sat up in his bed and continued, "You demon spirit, I recognize you. I cast you out earlier today. In the name of Jesus Christ of Nazareth, you *go now!*"

Dr. Sumrall told me that immediately the evil presence left the room. The heat returned, the curtains fell limply against the wall, the bed stopped shaking and the horrible odor left the room.

Now, did Brother Sumrall quietly lie back down to sleep? No! Instead he rose up in his bed, looked out the window and shouted, "Hey, devil. Get back in here!" Immediately the curtains began to stand out on end. Coldness filled the room. The horrible odor returned, and the bed began to shake so violently that it almost tossed him out on the floor.

He rose up in the bed and demanded, "Devil, when I came in this room, my bed was against that wall. Now in the name of Jesus, put it back!"

Immediately, his bed went back across the room and settled down against the wall. He sternly rebuked the evil presence and commanded it to leave. The demon left, and peace filled the night air.

In the following pages, we will move beyond repentance and refreshing. We will move into *restoration*. I will introduce you to and define restoration in three simple words, "Put it back!" The time has come for God's standard bearers to march as a terrible army under Christ's banner and demand of God's enemies, "Put it back!"

Put what back? Put back your joy. Put back your anointing. Put back your family. Put back your money. Put back your authority. Put back your shout. Put back your victory! Rebuke the devil and declare, "I am standing firm until you put back everything you have taken from me."

Taking It Back From the Enemy

"She looketh forth as the morning" (Song 6:10). Who is she? She is you and me! She is the church marching out to demand that the enemy put back everything he has stolen. We come forth as the morning with an atmosphere of expectancy, blowing with the wind of mighty miracles. We come forth each day, not dreading what the day holds but declaring,

> This is the day that the Lord hath made. I will rejoice and be glad in it. For if God is for me, who can be against me? A thousand shall fall at my side and ten thousand at my right hand but it shall not come nigh unto me. Of whom shall I be afraid if God is for me! (see Ps. 118:24; 91:7; 27:1; Rom. 8:31).

You think it's bad in the world today. Wait just a few short years until this planet finds out what it is like when God's standard bearers are not here restraining the forces of darkness through the power of the Holy Spirit.

Who is she? She is you and me — a terrible army with banners. All we have to do to strike fear and panic in the heart of our adversary is to invade his stolen territory and plant our own flag and lift high the emblem of our everlasting King.

We are standard bearers who are no longer satisfied with the desert in which we are living. A fresh breeze is blowing. The clouds are gathering. The rain is beginning to fall. The dry season of enemy domination is over. We are ready to recover spoils from our enemy. We want restoration!

We desire that His change be real — not just in our hearts but in our land as well. Satan has stolen what belongs to us, and we have lived without it long enough. We are gathering our forces and sharpening our sabers. We are ready to invade the enemy's territory and take back everything that rightfully belongs to us. We are raising high the blood-stained banner with the cross of Christ and declaring to the alien forces of the Antichrist that there's a Holy Spirit invasion taking place.

> A fresh breeze is blowing. The clouds are gathering. The rain is beginning to fall. The dry season of enemy domination is over. We are ready to recover spoils from our enemy. We want restoration!

Halfway between Guam and Japan sits a small island

named Iwo Jima. It's only five miles long and two-and-a-half miles at its widest point. During World War II it became the site of one of the bloodiest battles ever fought.

The Allied armies desperately needed Iwo Jima for their final assault on Japan. For several weeks they bombarded it day and night. Then, on February 19, 1945, the Fifth Marine Amphibious Corps stormed its beaches with six thousand determined soldiers in five hundred landing craft.

After seventy-two hours of relentless assault, our bloodied marines claimed victory on the southern end of the island. Four soldiers climbed to the top of Mount Suribachi and proudly planted the American flag. The photo of that moment was forever frozen in time. It is our most memorable image of World War II.

But the battle wasn't over. More than twenty thousand Japanese were hiding in an elaborate maze of caves and tunnels that spread through the northern half of the island. Our marines had no choice but to crawl into the caves and dig out the enemy one by one. In twenty-six days the battle was over. Four thousand helmets of slain marines were neatly stacked in remembrance, and over twenty thousand enemy lives were lost.

You and I are in the midst of a confrontation far greater than anything recorded in the annals of war — more devastating than the conflicts of Alexander the Great, Napoleon, Winston Churchill, Eisenhower or MacArthur. It is the battle of the ages fought on the fertile soil of the human heart. Tragically, too many lives have already been lost. The devil continues to wage an all-out offensive with only one objective: to see you disheartened and defeated.

What Are We Doing?

As the enemy attacks, what is the army of God, the bride of Christ, doing? Are we in position ready for the battle? Have we prepared to repel the attack under the banner of

Christ? I think not. Instead of taking our position on the battlefield, we have, like David, taken our position in the bedroom of our own lusts during a critical time of war (2 Sam. 11:1-4).

The land of the free and home of the brave has become the land of the socially acceptable and home of the faint-hearted.

The star-spangled banner is now a blazing spectacle ignited by First Amendment activists who are motivated by self-interest and sinful passion.

We have sacrificed the standards of righteousness and holiness for loose living and corrupt consciences. We have allowed Satan to move us from the realm of moral conservatism to the realm to moral liberalism.

> The land of the free and home of the brave has become the land of the socially acceptable and home of the fainthearted.

We have so immersed ourselves in political policies that we have forgotten Bible basics. We have sacrificed what is right on the altar of what is politically correct.

While the homosexuals are "coming out of the closet," Christians are "running to the closet" because they don't want to "clean out their closets."

We sing "Onward Christian Soldiers" safely behind the walls of our churches and claim authority in Christ but have no control over our own appetites.

We have traded the banner of the cross for a display of contempt; godly leadership for powerless men proclaiming the Word of God from the sewers of their drunken and adulterous lives; prayer for church politics; praise for perverse and profane idolatry; courage for cowardice; unity with God for fellowship with darkness; compassion for the lost for hostility toward hopeless humanity.

> We have traded the banner of the cross for a display of contempt... compassion for the lost for hostility toward hopeless humanity.

We have so lowered the standards of spiritual anointing that what we are now aiming for what was once under our feet. The prophet Isaiah, walking through the cobblestone streets of Jerusalem, loudly declared that truth lies fallen in the street (Is. 59:14).

Because of all this, rebellion against church leaders seems justified, and temptation to withdraw from fellowship is strong.

When irritation levels are high and patience is low, Satan comes to you in great wrath to destroy your life. He presents you with a multitude of inordinate fears and grotesque images which flash and burn in your imagination, draining you from peaceful and restful sleep. The enemy clouds your countenance with a dark cloud of oppression, leaving you more and more confused and disoriented.

When you see these things come to pass, know that spiritual wickedness in high places has come to destroy your life. It is time for your repentance, and time for God's refreshing and restoration in your life.

Come out of the desert. Leave behind the status quo. Declare an end to the dry seasons of your life. Lift high the standard of Christ against the enemy.

Remember, the Bible says, "When the enemy shall come in like a flood, the spirit of the Lord shall *lift up a standard* against him" (Is. 59:19, italics added).

In Iwo Jima, our fighting forces softened up the island by an aerial bombardment to prepare for digging out the enemy one by one. Like those marines, great generals of the faith such as Luther, Calvin, Wesley, Whitefield and Sunday have prepared the ground for us to reap the harvest. Some were sowing faith, and others were sowing healing. But at some point the sowing stops and the harvest begins, and we are that generation destined to overtake the sowers!

Raising a national banner will not help us. Lifting up a church banner cannot propel us. We must raise the banner of Christ, declaring the end to the dry seasons of God's people. The rain is falling, the rivers of God are flowing, and the harvest is ready!

We are not destined to scratch out a meager spiritual existence. We are not destined to pray prayers and allow three generations to pass before we reap the harvest. We are destined to invade the territory that has been softened up over the years, plunder our enemy and take back for the kingdom of God everything the enemy has stolen. We are destined to dig out all the devils that have been entrenched in our lives, homes and churches. The time of restoration is here!

> **After repentance comes the refreshing. Out of the refreshing, God brings forth restoration.**

After repentance comes the refreshing. Out of the refreshing, God brings forth restoration.

We are marching forth as an army of terrorists under the banner of Jesus Christ. We are going to invade enemy-held territory and take back what we lost. We are going to take

95

our churches back. We are going to take our neighborhoods back. I am tired of the drug lords selling crack on the streets to our kids. I am tired of the spirit of racism that is so dividing our churches and our nation. I want to see that all people from all ethnic backgrounds — Anglo and African American, Asian, Hispanic and Native American — march united as standard bearers under the banner of Christ.

"Terrible as an army with banners" refers to our response to the enemies of the cross, the enemies of the blood and the enemies of the church, all of which have an antichrist spirit and are in operation in the world today. If we believe we are the final generation, then we are going to have to learn how to deal with the spirit of antichrist.

What is the spirit of antichrist? It's some politician giving his address at the national convention with his mouth full of lies and his heart full of blackness. It's so-called community leaders who are pitting race against race with bigoted hatred. It is sickness and disease.

We are declaring war, marching as a terrible army with banners until Jesus comes back. Are you ready to march against the enemy and take back what he had no right to steal?

God Shall Send Jesus Christ

Repent ye, therefore, and be converted, that your sins may be blotted out, when the times of refreshing shall come from the presence of the Lord; and He shall send Jesus Christ, which before was preached unto you: Whom the heaven must receive until the times of restitution of all things, which God hath spoken by the mouth of all his holy prophets since the world began (Acts 3:19-21).

When will God send Jesus? God said, "I am holding My Son back until the restoration of all things." What is holding back His return?

In Matthew 24:3 the disciples ask Jesus two distinct questions:

- "Tell us, when shall these things be?"

- "What shall be the sign of thy coming, and of the end of the world?"

Jesus answers these questions separately. In answer to the first question He tells them about the things that will happen. These will be rumors of wars, famines, earthquakes and diseases. He warns of the false prophets that will arise and tells them that the love of many will grow cold.

After describing "these things," Jesus turns to answer the second question about the sign of His coming. Notice that He does not say "signs" but points to one overarching sign in Matthew 24:32-33.

> Now learn a parable of the fig tree; When his branch is yet tender, and putteth forth leaves, ye know that summer is nigh: so likewise ye, when ye shall see all these things, know that it is near, even at the doors.

Jesus is talking about one generation. A generation would begin when the fig tree puts forth her leaves. The fig tree is always symbolic of Israel. Two thousand years ago Jesus looked through the telescope of prophecy and said that when Israel became a nation again, we would know that we are moving toward the end of this world. The generation that was of age at that time would be the final generation. We are that generation!

The return of Jesus could not happen until God restored Israel as a nation. In A.D. 70, Jesus' prophecy was fulfilled: The temple was destroyed by Titus, and the Jews were scattered throughout the nations. But Israel was destined to be restored as a nation before a final generation would remain to see His return.

On May 15, 1948, a white flag with the blue star of David was recognized on the floor of the United Nations, and God in heaven let His judgment gavel come down. His clock began to wind down, and He said, "This is the generation that will see the coming of the great and terrible day of the Lord."

Somebody needs to wake us up. We have been playing around with popularity and meandering in a maze of mediocrity. We have failed to discern the day and the hour in which we are living. We are God's last great hope. But the good news is that He has saved the best for last. God's signs, wonders and power were awesome in the book of Acts, but we are destined to pass them like a space shuttle passing a covered wagon.

The sign given before the great and terrible day of the Lord is the restoration of Israel.

The Bible says restoration will not be fully realized until the Jews are gathered from the ends of the earth back to their homeland (Ezek. 36:24-28). In 1948 that had not yet happened. There was still a divided Jerusalem. Jerusalem was still being trodden underfoot by the gentiles.

Jesus said in Luke 21:24 that Jerusalem would be trodden down by the gentiles until the fullness of the gentiles is come. The "fulness of the gentiles" symbolizes the last generation that will exist on this planet before God takes the church in the rapture and begins seven years of determined dealings with the nation of Israel.

After the Six-Day War in 1967, Jerusalem was united and the Jewish people began to be gathered back to Israel as prophesied by Ezekiel. Since the collapse of the Soviet Union, over five hundred thousand Jews have left Russia and have been airlifted back into their homeland on the blue Mediterranean Sea.

Ten years ago the very thought of such a mass exodus couldn't have even been imagined. We thought the Jews never would get out. No one believed that the Berlin Wall would come down, that the U.S.S.R. would disintegrate, and that the Soviet republics would allow the Jews to leave in our generation. But today it is happening. Israel's restoration has begun. The clock is ticking, and Jesus is returning soon.

What are some of "these things" that Jesus predicted would happen right before the end? These are happening all around us — not just in some third world countries but in our own backyard!

Earthquakes on this planet have increased drastically in the last ten years.

Pestilence: One person in every 250 people living in this most prosperous and enlightened nation of the earth is infected with the HIV virus, and there is no cure. In 1995 it was the eighth leading cause of death in our nation. It was never heard of twenty years ago.

Wars happen around the earth with such regularity that we hardly notice anymore when fighting breaks out.

Rumors of wars fill our news broadcasts and papers.

Famine strikes even America, where we watch news documentaries that report on the children who are starving not only in Africa and in Asia but right here in our inner cities.

Jesus is returning soon!

Zechariah 14:12 foretells a time in the last days when great armies will march from the nations against Jerusalem, and God will smite them. "Their flesh shall consume away while they stand upon their feet, and their eyes shall consume away in their holes, and their tongue shall consume away in their mouth." Conventional warfare prior to the nuclear age never saw such destruction with guns, bayonets, grenades or machine guns. Not until this final generation have atomic bombs existed which can vaporize a person with millions of degrees of energy exploding in less than a second.

The book of Daniel reported that in the last days knowledge would increase. "But thou, O Daniel, shut up the words, and seal the book, even to the time of the end: many shall run to and fro, and knowledge shall be increased" (Dan. 12:4).

We don't even recognize how much it has increased. Computers, the Internet, microwaves, cellular telephones, modems, fax machines and other sophisticated devices have become commonplace. We cannot keep up with the expansion of knowledge all around us. Encyclopedias are no longer just volumes of books but data stored on a CD-ROM.

In the last one hundred years transportation has become so advanced that it no longer takes days to travel from one city to another. Now we can travel from New York City to London on a Concorde jet in less than three hours.

Medical knowledge is exploding. Doctors with the aid of life-support systems can keep critically ill people alive for months or years.

In the midst of all these things happening before the end of time, what good news is there? The good news is restoration. The good news is that God is going to use a restored, mighty church to come forth as the morning.

The Church — Completely Restored

God declared in Joel 2:25, "I will restore to you the years that the locust hath eaten, the cankerworm, and the caterpillar, and the palmerworm." There has been an eating, a gnawing away at the basic tenets of the faith. Satan has schemed, planned and connived for centuries to rob the church of her God-ordained gifts, and he has been successful at invading our pulpits and our pews with stale, dead religion void of power and void of God.

Compromise, conformity and selfish motives have produced a spiritually empty church. But before the great and terrible day of the Lord we have this guarantee: God will restore to the church her gifts, anointing, ministry and anything else she requires to become His glorious bride without spot or blemish (Eph. 5:27).

Before Jesus comes He will restore the church to new life. There won't be any more powerless preachers trying to preach the gospel out of the sinfulness of their lives. There won't be any more saints who pray without the manifestation of God's power. God is going to straighten us out!

A time of restoration is upon us in the church. The sign of His coming is at hand: Israel is a nation. The signs before the end are all around us: Rumors of wars, earthquakes, pestilences and famine.

What else happens before the end? Acts 3:19-21 clearly reveals that "times of refreshing shall come from the presence of the Lord; and he shall send Jesus Christ...Whom the heaven must receive until the times of restitution of all things, which God hath spoken by the mouth of all his holy prophets since the world began." Refreshing and restoration are to happen *before* Jesus returns.

There is a new day dawning just over the horizon! In Joel 2:19 God promised, "Behold, I will send you corn, and wine, and oil, and ye shall be satisfied therewith: and I will no more make you a reproach among the heathen." In the past the church has been looked upon with scorn and disdain because she lacked the power and spiritual armor to withstand even the smallest onslaught of Satanic attack. But this verse says that our corn, wine and oil will be restored.

- Corn represents the Word of God.

With the banner of God's Word we, the church, will once again blaze the trail of gospel truth and march to the forefront in His strength and power to recover our ministry and authority.

- Oil represents the Holy Spirit.

The wind, fire, power and anointing of the Holy Spirit will be manifested in our churches and in our lives, producing mighty miracles and pointing to the cross of Calvary. We will again be known as a body which is ready to walk under the command of Jesus.

- Wine represents joy.

The wine or joy of the gospel will be returned to us. Things in this world are not getting better; they are getting worse. Our only hope is in living for, trusting in and obeying God and His Word. He will give us a song to sing at midnight when trouble seems to be closing in all around. Nothing shall be able rob us of our joy in Christ (John 16:22).

Wine, oil and corn do not flow and grow in dry land. They are the fruits of the fresh rain of God falling on the prepared soil of God's people. Plow the dry land. Pray in the rain. Cultivate the wine, oil and corn. Bring in an abundant harvest from the Lord.

Lost — At Home

There is a stirring in the church today. Why? She is looking for something. What is she searching for? Like the woman in Luke 15:8-9 she is looking for what she lost:

Either what woman having ten pieces of silver, if

she lose one piece, doth not light a candle, and
sweep the house, and seek diligently till she find it?
And when she hath found it, she called her friends
and her neighbors together, saying, Rejoice with
me; for I have found the piece which I had lost.

This woman was very dignified. She was a picture of the
New Testament church on the day of Pentecost, wearing
gifts, power, authority and anointing. But the Bible says she
lost something. She misplaced something very dear and
precious to her. She lost a coin — her treasure.

She entered a dry season in her life. When the things of
God which are precious to us become ordinary, we soon
replace them. But then, like the woman who lost a coin,
we yearn after, long for and miss our treasure. We begin to
inspect our lives and find that something just doesn't seem
right.

What do we do? What did the woman do? First, *she swept
her house.* The first thing this woman did in search of her
coin was to sweep her house. She didn't go out into the
streets; she didn't go to work; she didn't go to her neighbor's, friend's or family's houses. She swept her own house.
Everything that you lost, everything that you need is in one
place — right in your house. Look for great changes in your
life! God is about to rush through your life. He is about to
help you discover some misplaced treasures in your life.

Some in the body of Christ are now getting serious about
what they have lost. They are ready to go forth into the
morning and reclaim what has been lost in the dark. They
are no longer content to wander in the desert and remain
dry and parched. They are crying out for the rain of God.
Some people are now getting serious about prayer. Some
are getting serious about studying the Bible, going to
church and manifesting the gifts of the Holy Spirit. There is
a group of people, a remnant, getting serious about taking

back their family, their finances and everything else that has been stolen.

She lit a candle and went looking. In order to find what is lost we must light the candle of the Word of God and allow it to illuminate the darkest recesses of our hearts.

The church is being restored to the Word of God. We must plant our feet in the Bible, turn a deaf ear to the world and proclaim, "I am not leaving until everything is restored to me. I don't have time for your gossip. I don't have time for your doubt and unbelief. I am searching for something, and in the name of Jesus I won't stop until I find it!"

The restored church that looketh forth into the morning, fair as the moon and clear as the sun, can march as a terrible army when she knows where to look for what she is missing. Have you lost your joy? You can find it. It's in there. It's in the Word. Have you lost your victory? You can have victory. Again, it's in the Word!

For decades the church has been wandering around in the dark looking for what she has lost, aimlessly treking through the desert looking for water, but no more! The light is on. The rain is falling. The morning has come! We have our glorious light and living water for the march — God's Word.

Like Lester Sumrall, we are ordering the devil to put everything back. We know our authority as the saints of the most high God. We are taking back what the enemy has devoured and destroyed. The naysayers and your religious friends may try to tell you it cannot be done, but the Bible says that we can do all things through Christ who strengthens us (Phil. 4:13).

Mary Magdalene and the other women in Matthew 28 went looking for something they had lost — their Savior. They heard He was in the garden tomb. They rose up early in the morning. They brought some gifts with them. You take gifts to somebody when you expect to see them. They brought Him a gift. They went looking for Him. They didn't find Him, but they met an angel, and the angel told them not to fear. He essentially said, "I know who you are looking for — Jesus, He's not here. He's out on a stroll" (see Matt. 28:5-6). Mary Magdalene went looking for Jesus through her tears. She was serious about finding Him.

In 1 Samuel 30 we read the story of the armies of the Amalekites who invaded and burned the town of Ziklag to the ground. David and his men came upon the torched city and found that their women, children and possessions had been carried off as spoils of war. But the Bible says that David encouraged himself in the Lord and inquired of Him, "Shall I pursue after this troop? Shall I overtake them?" And the Lord answered him, "Pursue: for thou shalt surely overtake them, and without fail *recover all*" (v. 8, italics added). Are you seriously looking to have restored to you what you have lost?

You may be saying to yourself, *I've lost something. I must find it again. I've lost my anointing. I'm supposed to be treading on serpents, and they are treading on me. I've lost something. I'm supposed to have joy. I'm crying all the time. I've lost something. I used to have passion, but I feel numb inside. I've lost the flow from the fountain of living water within me. I'm in a dry season. I've lost something. I have to find it.*

The Bible says concerning Job, "The Lord blessed the latter end of Job more than his beginning" (Job 42:12). He is the restorer. He will help you find things. He will put things back where they used to be.

Restored, We Are Coming Out of Egypt!

Joel 2:23 says, "For he hath given you the former rain moderately, and he will cause to come down for you the rain, the former rain, and the latter rain in the first month."

As I stated at the beginning of this chapter, we are going to reap where we did not sow. We, the reapers, are going to overtake the sowers. We are the generation destined for the experiential manifestation of the glory of God.

Here is a tremendous parallel. Go back with me to Egypt. Do you remember when God brought the Israelites out of Egyptian bondage? He said, "Before you leave I am going to restore to you some things you have lost." During their years of slavery, working for the advancement of their hard taskmasters, they lost some things. But God promised that he was going to deliver them from the evil Pharaoh into their own land. Always remember, when God delivers you *from* something, He always delivers you *to* something else, and it is always something better.

Exodus 12:31 says, "And he [Pharaoh] called for Moses and Aaron by night, and said, Rise up, and get you forth from among my people, both ye and the children of Israel; and go, serve the Lord, as ye have said." Pharaoh in so many words told Moses, "I have had about as much of you as I can stand."

That is the way the devil is going to be with us! He will be anxious to turn us loose. Look at what the Bible says happened next:

> And the Egyptians were urgent upon the people, that they might send them out of the land in haste; for they said, We be all dead men...And the children of Israel did according to the word of Moses; and they borrowed [demanded] of the Egyptians jewels of silver, and jewels of gold, and raiment: And the Lord gave the people favour in the sight of the Egyptians, so that they lent unto them such things as they required. And they spoiled the Egyptians (Ex. 12:33,35-36).

The Hebrew word for *borrowed* in verse 34 means

demanded. The Israelites turned the tables on Pharaoh and basically told him, "If you want us to leave so bad, you are going to have to give us something. You are going to have to restore some things to us. Give us back our children, give us back our flocks and herds, give us some clothes, and don't forget to give us some money!" So Pharaoh loaded them up, sent them on their way and asked them to bless him before they left.

Wouldn't that be something — your enemies asking you to bless them! Before the return of Jesus, God is going to give you favor. He is going to cause your enemies to be at peace with you. Those who have cursed you, He will cause to bless you. Psalm 5:12 says, "For thou, Lord, wilt bless the righteous; with favour wilt thou compass him as with a shield." Those who have betrayed you, laughed at you and mocked you are going to bow their knees at the spout where the glory of God comes out of your life. God will prepare a table before you in the presence of your enemies and make them provide the food too!

God is also going to restore health to your body as He did to the bodies of the Israelites. Psalm 105:37 reveals, "He brought them forth also with silver and gold: and there was not one feeble person among their tribes." Do you notice what God did? He healed every person. I know it is hard to comprehend. Perhaps your body has been wracked with pain, arthritis or disease for many years. But the Bible says they were *all* restored to health. There weren't any eyeglasses, hearing aids, canes, wheelchairs or walkers. There wasn't any heart disease; there were no tumors or cancer. God healed every earache, every headache and every backache. Before Jesus splits the eastern sky and comes in His magnificent magnitude, I believe every single person in the church is going to be healed.

We will recover wealth. The church of Jesus Christ is not going to leave this planet deprived and full of debt! In order to fulfill the Great Commission we must have money. In order to preach the gospel through the medium of television and shortwave radio to lost and hurting people around the world we must have more than just a few crumpled-up one-dollar bills. Before you can pay for your children's Christian education, your mortgage or your doctor bills you need money.

And like the Egyptians did to the Israelites, the world is going to heap on us and the church so much wealth that we are going to be able to dig out of debt and have money left over to spread the gospel message! "The wealth of the sinner is laid up for the just" (Prov. 13:22).

Here is another important verse of scripture. James 5:1-3 says:

> Go to now, ye rich men, weep and howl for your miseries that shall come upon you. Your riches are corrupted, and your garments are motheaten. Your gold and silver is cankered; and the rust of them shall be a witness against you, and shall eat your flesh as it were fire. Ye have heaped treasure together for the last days.

There are vast pockets of wealth on this planet that will stagger your mind. In my father's generation there were only a few millionaires and just a handful of billionaires. But today they are everywhere. The world is heaping up treasure for the last days. But James says for rich men to get ready to weep and howl.

In James 5:7 he continues, but now he is talking to the church, "Be patient therefore, brethren, unto the coming of the Lord. Behold, the husbandman waiteth for the precious fruit of the earth, and hath long patience for it, until he receive the early and latter rain." What is He saying? He is saying, just be patient. The early and the latter rain are going to come forth in one month in the fig tree generation, our generation, and it is going to rain down everything the devil has stolen: Our wealth, our health, *everything!*

Here is the last perfect parallel between our generation and the generation that came out of Egyptian bondage. Do you remember the final plague pronounced upon the Egyptians before they were allowed to leave? Every first-born of the household of Egypt, including those of their flocks, were slain. But the angel of death passed over the Israelites when the blood was applied to their doorposts. The blood was applied in the form of a cross, foreshadowing the redemptive power of Jesus' blood (see Ex. 12:21-23,29-30). Not only were they given favor, health and wealth, but they did not experience death.

So it is with the restoration of the church. There is only one group of people who are not going to leave this planet through the agency of death. Who are they? They are those who exit this planet in the rapture. They are not going to be buried; they are going to be changed.

First Thessalonians 4:17 says, "Then we which are alive and remain shall be caught up together with them in the clouds, to meet the Lord in the air: and so shall we ever be with the Lord." We are going to be like Enoch. One moment we will be here, and the next we will be gone, shouting in the words of Dr. Lester Sumrall, "Good-bye, world! So long, planet earth! It's been nice knowing you!"

So, church, look forth into the morning. We must stop wandering around as though we were lost in the dark. Receive your restoration in Christ Jesus. Just as the thief must restore sevenfold, so must the devil deliver into our hands seven times more than what he has stolen (Prov. 6:31).

Jesus is restoring the church now. She is coming forth into the morning, fair as the moon and clear as the sun. As a terrible army with banners, the restored church will lift high the banner of Christ. She comes forth as a restored church with a sevenfold blessing.

Pray:

> *Lord, I didn't say it, but You did. You saved the best wine for last. I am ready for the restoration of the Word, anointing and joy. I receive the restoration of everything the devil has stolen from me. I take back my health. I take back my finances. I take back my family. I thank you because if the thief be found, he must restore sevenfold everything he has taken. It is mine now! Amen.*

Section II

Heed the Call

Across the misty plains of time, a voice reaches from the shores of Galilee to this land. The voice sounds as a trumpet, rings as a carillon, roars as the thunder and crashes as towering breakers along a jagged, rocky shore.

Unmistakable...that voice. With a word, that voice brought galaxies into being; raised corpses from the dead; pronounced healing to all who listened; spoke judgment to every two-faced hypocrite; and comforted the lost and distraught.

Now, that same voice comes as a still, small voice; as the sound of rushing rivers; as the balm of Gilead; as the conviction of the deepest truth; and as the command for countless legions. Hear that voice: "Take up your cross and follow me."

Dare we heed the call? Why do I ask? Because what we freely receive cost Him dearly. The price was paid on the cross. With His back fileted into ribbons and blood streaming down an unrecognizable face, the Speaker of that voice uttered words paid for with His suffering and death, "Father, forgive them." Out of nail-pierced hands, spike-punctured feet and a dagger-torn side gushed the cleansing flood of Emmanuel's blood. The call issued from His lips cost Him everything. From before the foundation of the world, He was slain that we might live.

Do you hear the voice?

It is not the voice of rules,
   regulations,
     restrictions,
       religions
         and requirements.

It is not the voice of a preacher or a choir,
   an evangelist or a television star.

It is not the voice of a politician or a president,
   of a tycoon or a CEO.

We first heard the voice as a baby's cry. Surprised, we came as shepherds and wise men to check His credentials and inspect His ancestry. The voice seemed normal enough, but that in itself threw us off. We had become so abnormal that the sound of normalcy was strange to our ears. We expected an emperor's edict, not a voice crying in a stable. We listened for the resonance of an educated rabbi schooled in the traditions of Hillel or Gamaliel, not the dialect of a Galilean without so much as a degree or a certificate.

And then, when the voice spoke directly to us, we

recoiled, startled and offended by words that cut as two-
edged swords to the depths of our hearts.
The voice cried, "Repent."
  And we asked, "When?"

The voice demanded, "Now."
  And we asked, "Why?"

The voice invited, "Follow me."
    And we entreated, "But first..."

The voice instructed, "He who loses his life will find it."
  And we protested, "But my life is all I have."

The voice revealed, "He who is great, let him serve."
  And we excused ourselves, "I can't serve because..."

The voice has been
  muffled by the noises of this world,
    obscured by the clamor of our inner, competing lusts,
      blocked by the dampers of our sinful bondages,
        distorted by the frequencies of our compromises.

  Nevertheless, the voice speaks to us now — and we must
listen.
  Why? Because eternity hinges upon our both hearing
and heeding the call.

Whose is the voice?
  The voice is of One who is both Lion and Lamb;
    both Servant and King;
      both Crucified and Alive;
      both Man and God.

  The voice is not a word *from* God, but the Word *of* God.
        To what are we called?

NO DRY SEASON

Called to Wholeness.
Called to Win.
Called to Worship.
Called to Warning.

Fly the banner...plant the flag...raise the standard.

Dare we heed the call?
As standard bearers, we can follow no other voice and
heed no other call.

Read on, you who goeth forth as the morning,
fair as the moon,
clear as the sun,
terrible as an army with banners.

Let these coming pages be a wake-up call,
an emergency call,
a warning call,
an urgent call,
an interrupting call.

Stop all that you are doing.
Read, meditate, fast and pray.
Then...
Heed the call!

6

Called to Wholeness

Your lives are echoing the Master's Word" (1 Thess. 1:8, *The Message*). What a powerful description of standard bearers and of how the church goes forth as a terrible army under the banner of Christ!

I am privileged to have been raised by godly parents, and today our relationship is stronger and better than ever. One thing I love to do is hunt with my dad. When we go deer hunting, he particularly likes to hunt with a Weatherby 7mm magnum rifle. When we head into the woods, he says, "When you hear the big 7mm crack, come running, because the meal will be on the ground, and I don't want to pull him out myself."

When Dad shoots his gun in the mountains, you can hear the sound of the shot wash down the sides of the hills. The noise can be heard for miles as it thunders around you and ripples through the trees. Now that's an echo. That's reverberation.

"Who is she that looketh forth as the morning...terrible as an army with banners?" (Song 6:10). She is a church called to wholeness and made up of standard bearers whose lives reverberate with the gospel of Jesus Christ. Reverberation is not just one echo. To reverberate is to re-echo, to resound with the noise of something over and over again.

She is a whole, united church taking the gospel to city hall. But the Word doesn't stop there. The Word reverberates! From city hall it echoes to the inner city. From the inner city it echoes to the suburbs and countryside. From the city street, the gospel echoes to the expressway. From the expressway the Word reverberates down the county roads and the interstates and shakes even the dirt roads and gravel paths.

Listen to this word of reverberation from 1 Thessalonians 1:5-8 in *The Message:*

> When the Message we preached came to you, it wasn't just words. Something happened in you. The Holy Spirit put steel in your convictions. You paid careful attention to the way we lived among you...you imitated the Master. Although great trouble accompanied the Word, you were able to take great joy from the Holy Spirit! — taking the trouble with the joy, the joy with the trouble...Your lives are echoing the Master's Word, not only in the provinces but all over the place. The news of your faith in God is out. We don't even have to say anything anymore — you're the message!

How does the church echo the Master's Word? How does a standard bearer heed God's call to wholeness, unity and love? A sound echoing off many different standards would

116

simply be noise, confusion and clamour. But when there is one Master, one Commander-in-Chief, one gospel, one Word and one body, then the reverberation that comes from the whole people of God will wash through the land with the sound of good news from the throne of God.

There are three ways we reverberate or echo the Master's Word in heeding God's call to wholeness in the body of Christ. The Thessalonians were effective standard bearers in their day because they reverberated in these areas: their work of faith, labor of love, and patience of hope in Christ (1 Thess. 1:3). Let's look at how these three qualities both unify and equip us to heed the call of wholeness as God's standard bearers in the church.

1. Do Your Work of Faith

"You deserted the idols of your old life so you could embrace and serve God, the true God" (1 Thess. 1:9, *The Message*). A separation is coming for the church and her standard bearers. We separate ourselves from worldliness unto holiness.

The standard bearer cannot be of the world. Yes, we live in the world for the purpose of being salt, light and even a consuming fire blazing for Christ. Still, we live lives separate from the world's standard. We raise high the standard of Christ, not the standard of MTV or Wall Street or main street. We do not reverberate the message coming out of Washington. We echo the Master's Word.

Paul is not talking about the work that the Thessalonians were doing as a result of faith. He is speaking about the work of faith which caused them to become regenerated, born-again believers. That work of faith caused them to leave their dead idols.

The church's call to wholeness begins with a call to the one God. "Hear, O Israel: The Lord our God is one Lord: and thou shalt love the Lord thy God with all thine heart, and with all thy soul, and with all thy might" (Deut. 6:4-5). A whole, united church cannot have divided loyalties and loves.

> There must be an absolute destruction of the worldly gods that we have paid homage to in the church. We must slaughter every holy cow. God demands of us righteousness.

There must be an absolute destruction of the worldly gods that we have paid homage to in the church. We must slaughter every holy cow. God demands of us righteousness.

Righteousness is not what you do. It is the work of faith in you that takes place after God has resurrected Himself on the inside of you. He deposits His holiness in you after burning out and purging from you every past idol. His consuming fire destroys your idols. That's the work of faith within you.

We are called to unity and wholeness in righteousness. That righteousness in Christ so binds us together that those who fight against us find themselves fighting against God. We go forth into the morning under the banner of Christ. Jesus declared, "He that is not with me is against me; and he that gathereth not with me scattereth abroad" (Matt. 12:30). Romans 8:31 asserts, "If God be for us, who can be against us? Christ is our righteousness" (1 Cor. 1:30). We have been separated from the world by the righteousness of Christ Jesus.

A separation or demarcation from the world happens when the church draws a line in the sand and says resolutely, "We will not cross over into the world. We will not stand on the edge." Too many church people are playing games with God. Instead of turning their back on the world and its idols, they try to walk as close to the edge between the world and holiness as they can without falling. Don't just compromise! Turn your back on the world and walk away from it. Stop trying to see how much you can get away with and still be a Christian. Go all out for the kingdom of God with complete abandonment of the world's idols.

We must stand head and shoulders above the world as the righteous elect of God Almighty. Unity begins with holiness, righteousness and separation from the world.

> And what agreement hath the temple of God with idols? for ye are the temple of the living God; as God hath said, I will dwell in them, and walk in them; and I will be their God, and they shall be my people. Wherefore come out from among them, and be ye separate, saith the Lord, and touch not the unclean thing; and I will receive you (2 Cor. 6:16-17).

We must reverberate His holiness into a world that's desperately in need of the gospel. We must lift high the standard of His righteousness!

When God's work of faith in us produces His righteousness, then His healing power will reverberate in our lives. Why? Because we are living holy lives. Righteousness will bring down the idols of addiction, homosexuality, immorality and every form of abomination. Healing, deliverance, repentance, refreshing and restoration will reverberate from our lives and invade the world. Even the "little idols" in our lives will come under the scrutinizing light of God's Word. He will expose the excesses in our lives and the things we say we can't live without and require us to lay them down.

His work of faith in standard bearers will produce a sensitivity to His voice. When we hear Him speak, "Destroy that idol in your life," we will obey. We will be quick to repent and turn away from the world. Holy Spirit power will reverberate in our beings, shaking us to the core and loosing the grip of every worldly thing in our lives.

> # Before the church turns the world upside down with the gospel of Jesus Christ, God will first shake everything that can be shaken in our lives.

Before the church turns the world upside down with the gospel of Jesus Christ, God will first shake everything that can be shaken in our lives. He will tear down every idol that distracts us from being the standard bearers of Christ.

And this word, yet once more, signifieth the removing of those things that are shaken, as of things that are made [man-made idols], that those things which cannot be shaken may remain. Wherefore we receiving a kingdom which cannot be moved, let us have grace, whereby we may serve God acceptably with reverence and godly fear: For our God is a consuming fire (Heb. 12:27-29).

The work of faith within the church's call to wholeness will shake us from every idol so that we may fix our eyes on Jesus alone. Is His faith at work in you? Are you heeding His call to separate yourself from the world and become unified within the body of Christ? Is His righteousness destroying every idol that pulls you away from His plan for your life? Pray:

Lord, perform your work of faith in me that I

*might be shaken and separated from every
idol and might live righteously for you. Amen.*

2. Make Love the Inspiration of Your Labor

If you are to heed His call to wholeness, the work of
faith will cause you to leave every idol. For what? For your
labor of love. What is that labor of love? Service. No longer
will the world's principle of 20/80 apply to the church. In
the world 20 percent of the people in an organization do
all the giving and all the work while 80 percent sit around
watching the rest serve. Not
so in God's terrible army
going forth as the morning
under Christ's banner.

God's response to the work
of faith in you is to produce
His labor of love through you.

As you leave idols, sepa-
rate yourself from the world
and live righteously, God
responds by releasing His

> God's response to the work of faith in you is to produce His labor of love through you.

life and His living waters in you. His life is love, and that
love is the inspiration for our labor, work and service in the
kingdom of God.

I labor for Christ because I love Him. That love isn't
something I have produced. Rather, the love in me is a fruit
of the Holy Spirit (Gal. 5:22). God's life flowing out of me
produces the love I need to labor effectively for Him. God's
life in me is not a hate life or a critical life. In fact, His love
flowing out of me into others becomes a well of refreshing
for them. This is the power of the gospel:

- "For God so *loved* the world" (John 3:16, italics
  added).

- "That Christ may dwell in your hearts by faith; that ye, being rooted and grounded in *love,* may be able to comprehend with all saints what is the breadth, and length, and depth, and height; and to know the *love* of Christ" (Eph. 3:17-19, italics added).

- "Beloved, let us *love* one another: for *love* is of God.... He that *loveth* not knoweth not God; for God is *love"* (1 John 4:7-8, italics added).

How does a church called to wholeness labor in love? We pick people up instead of pushing them down. We build up rather than destroying. We offer a cup of water in Jesus' name. When people fall, we don't kick them when they are down. We circle the wagons around them to protect and nurture them. We don't shoot our wounded. We forgive and restore in the name of Jesus.

I've seen the labor of love in my own church. People will mow an elderly person's lawn in 110° weather when their own lawn is overgrown. Staff will work harder as a result of this love than anyone in a secular job ever does. People will work in the nursery or the food bank — not out of duty but out of love. Love should be the inspiration of labor in the church.

In Matthew 19 Jesus puts it simply and bluntly: "Love your neighbor" (NIV). Do you want revival in your neighbor? Do you want to refresh others with living water? Do you want to heed the call to wholeness in the church? Do you want your labor to count for eternity? Then love your neighbor.

God's love must so reverberate in our relationships that we reach the point where the spirits of this world fall off us and the Spirit of love permeates all that we do and say. Jesus declares that the way the world knows we are His disciples is by our love. "By this shall all men know that ye are my disciples, if ye have love one to another" (John 13:35).

Build horizontal love relationships.

When we heed the call to wholeness, we build relationships of love vertically with God and horizontally with one another. Wholeness and unity are built with *agape,* uncon ditional love — God's kind of love. It is a love that gives without expecting to receive. *Agape* is given without any expectation of gratitude or recognition.

Here's the power of the gospel: Love People.

Here's the power of the gospel: Love People.

Loving means accepting people whom tradition and religion tell us to reject. I remember the first time my Uncle Willie came to our church. For thirty-five years not a single day that went by that he wasn't drunk. The day he first came to church he was drunk and his clothes were all ragged and dirty. All Willie knew was that there was a church standing in the middle of a cornfield that said, "Send me your poor. Send me your hurting, huddled masses, and they will not be ridiculed or rejected. They will be loved with an unconditional love that inspires labor."

It's time for the church not only to accept the unlovable who come to her but also to go out seeking the unlovely. We need to find people to love! As standard bearers we have God's banner of love waving over us. Everyone can see that we are loved and are walking in love.

Start in your own family. Love that husband or wife who at times is hard to love. Love that teenager who seems distant and rebellious. Love somebody; care about somebody; hurt for somebody!

I pray that the time comes when the church heeds the call of love to such a degree that we wake up in the middle of the night with someone on our hearts and begin to intercede for him. I pray that we begin fasting meals and giving the money we would have spent on the meals to feed hungry and starving people. I pray that we will get up early on Sunday morning to pick up someone who cannot drive and who desires to go to church.

We are to love God with all that we are, and then to love our neighbors as ourselves. Who is our neighbor? The word for *neighbor* comes from two words meaning "dwelling" and "near." Anyone dwelling near you is your neighbor. He may be living in a shack or a penthouse. He may be an alcoholic or a drug dealer. He may be from the inner city or the suburbs.

Take to heart Paul's words, "For in Jesus Christ neither circumcision availeth any thing, nor uncircumcision; but faith which worketh by love" (Gal. 5:6). In others words, faith doesn't find its expression in religious acts but in acts of love. James declares, "If ye fulfill the royal law according to the scripture, Thou shalt love thy neighbour as thyself, ye do well" (2:8).

Husbands and wives need to stop hurting one another and start spending time each day serving one another in love. Instead of demanding their rights, spouses should look for ways to submit to one another and serve one another as unto the Lord.

To love others, we must surrender our right to be right.

To love others, we must surrender our right to be right.

Oh, I have heard all the protests coming from marriages and homes. "Pastor, you should hear the way they treat me. I have the right to be bitter and angry." Some of God's people are filled with unforgiveness, bitterness, anger and strife. If you've been forgiven by Christ, then forgive. God's Word clearly states, "And be ye kind one to another, tenderhearted, forgiving one another, even as God for Christ's sake hath forgiven you" (Eph. 4:32).

I love taking my little girl to the ice cream parlor on a date. We spend time together. Parents need to take time out for their children. What we buy them isn't nearly as important as the time we spend with them. Some parents have no relationship at all with their kids, and they blame their kids. Take them back from the enemy! Get face-to-face with them and spend time with them. Refuse to let your children withdraw into the world.

God's people need to spend time together in prayer, studying the Word, fellowshiping and just having fun. Take time for your friends in Christ. Be there for one another.

Some Christians have no relationship with their coworkers. They have been hurt and wounded and are using that as an excuse not to build relationships. If you are one of these, get over it! Relationships can hurt, but they are worth it. Forgiving people reverberates God's love in their lives.

The Bible needs to be applied and put into practice in all of our horizontal relationships. We need to edify and exhort and extend mercy, grace and forgiveness. Since we have received so much grace, we need to give it and share it. At times, a horizontal relationship can be saved with just three words, "I am sorry." And what about the word *honor?* We are to "honor others above ourselves" (Phil. 2:3; Rom. 12:10). Put these words into practice in your relationships!

Some think that gospel power lies in laying hands on the sick, experiencing manifestations of the Spirit, prophesying, big buildings, programs or choirs. However, Jesus points to love as the ultimate power of the gospel.

> Herein is my Father glorified, that ye bear much fruit; so shall ye be my disciples. As the Father hath loved me, so have I loved you: continue ye in my love...This is my commandment, that ye

love one another, as I have loved you (John 15:8-9,12).

Build your vertical love relationship through serving God.

How is your prayer life? When was the last time you stayed alone in prayer until you were not alone anymore? How in love are you with God's Word?

Our relationship with God must grow continually. Prayer, loving the Word, confession, speaking forth the things of God and allowing our lives to be permeated with love for Him are all part of expanding our vertical relationship with God. Our idols must die. We must fall in love and stay in love with Jesus. He is our first love.

The three keys to building our vertical love relationship with God are prayer, the Word and worship. A church service cannot be the only time during the week when we express our love to God. When prayer, the Word and worship are expressed in a daily love relationship with the Father, then our church worship as a body will explode with praise and power. Powerless worship reflects powerless lives lived daily without God.

Too many church people live lives as practical atheists. They dance, sing, shout and pray in tongues in the church building, but their lives are nothing more than vacant tabernacles. You will never minister to God in corporate worship until you begin ministering to Him daily through personal worship, prayer and time in the Word.

3. Be Patient and Filled With Hope

Patience is not a passive word; *patience* is an active word. We are going to wait. How are we going to wait? Reaping. We will expend our energies winning others to Christ in the time we have left on this planet. God can use us to reach out to somebody who is going to hell if we have the patience to wait on Him.

Patience does not mean sitting around polishing our armor and repairing our banners. We are here to win the lost to Jesus Christ. He is our hope, the only hope we have to share with a lost and dying world. Take an unsaved family member to dinner. Serve that person. Love and minister the grace of God to that person. Echo Christ's love in your life to the lost. When we are patient until the coming of the Lord, working to bring in the harvest, revival will explode in our midst.

Ten Keys to Heeding God's Call to Wholeness

Notice that reverberation, righteousness and relationships are all part of God's call to wholeness for the church. Let me share with you some very practical ways your life as a standard bearer can reverberate with God's righteousness and love.

1. Finish what you have started.

Have you started praying and reading the Word daily? Keep doing it. Have you started a relationship that needs to grow? Continue on. "Therefore, my beloved brethren, be ye steadfast, unmoveable, always abounding in the work of the Lord, forasmuch as ye know that your labour is not in vain in the Lord" (1 Cor. 15:58).

2. Don't let your good intentions grow stale.

Never grow tired of well-doing. Does someone need to hear from you about Christ? Witness. Is someone sick, in prison, poor or hungry? Serve the least of these in Jesus' name. "And let us not be weary in well doing: for in due season we shall reap, if we faint not" (Gal. 6:9).

3. Guard your heart.

Keep your heart in the right place. Deposit the Word of God in your heart to keep from sinning against God. "Keep thy heart with all diligence; for out of it are the issues of life" (Prov. 4:23).

4. Act in faith now on what you know.

Stop filling notebook after notebook with information about God's Word. Act upon the Word that you know. Apply the eternal truths of God in your daily life. Don't sit, soak and sour. To hear God's Word means to do it. Seek, search out and serve the Lord. "But be ye doers of the word, and not hearers only, deceiving your own selves" (James 1:22).

5. Commit and complete the task.

Don't just do half of your service to God. Love and serve others with excellence. Finish the devil off. Don't let him off the hook. Go beyond just rebuking him — defeat him and drive him completely out of your life and your relationships. "Wherefore seeing we also are compassed about with so great a cloud of witnesses, let us lay aside every weight, and the sin which doth so easily beset us, and let us run with patience the race that is set before us, looking unto Jesus the author and finisher of our faith" (Heb. 12:1-2).

6. Go with God.

When God gives you the green light, stop praying about it and go with the wind of the Holy Spirit. Too often Christians know God's will but continue to pray about their situation. Stop restricting the flow of living water out of your life. Get yourself out of the way and allow the Holy

Spirit to guide, direct and empower you to do His will. "Be filled with the Spirit" (Eph. 5:18).

7. Resist the spirit of this age.

Don't associate with ungodly people. Refuse to surround yourself with critical, restless, skeptical people. Seek out those who love Jesus and others. Be encouraged by victors instead of discouraged by victims. "Blessed is the man that walketh not in the counsel of the ungodly, nor standeth in the way of sinners, nor sitteth in the seat of the scornful. But his delight is in the law of the Lord; and in his law doth he meditate day and night. And he shall be like a tree planted by the rivers of water, that bringeth forth his fruit in his season; his leaf also shall not wither; and whatsoever he doeth shall prosper" (Psalm 1:1-3).

8. Do what you can — not what you can't.

You can do all things through Christ who strengthens you. Stop focusing on your problems and fix your eyes on the problem solver — Jesus Christ. Seek service not status. Use the gifts God gave you without envying the gifts of others. Find your place as a member of the body of Christ, and stay there serving humbly. Replace performing for Christ with seeking to please Him with service. Remember, you serve and worship an audience of One. "Forgetting those things which are behind, and reaching forth unto those things which are before, I press toward the mark for the prize of the high calling of God in Christ Jesus...I can do all things through Christ which strengtheneth me" (Phil. 3:13-14; 4:13).

9. Let your heart control your hands.

God will give you a new heart and fulfill the desires of

your heart. Remember that without a vision, God's people perish in the desert of old, stopped-up wells. Your vision is His. Don't ask Him to bless your plan. Ask Him for His plan that you might be blessed. "Where there is no vision, the people perish: but he that keepeth the law, happy is he" (Prov. 29:18).

    10. Work shoulder-to-shoulder in unity with other standard bearers.

When two agree in prayer, heaven is moved. One chases a thousand, and two put ten thousand to flight (Deut. 32:30). "Again I say unto you, That if two of you shall agree on earth as touching any thing that they shall ask, it shall be done for them of my Father which is in heaven" (Matt. 18:19).

God worked mighty signs and wonders through the early church because they were of one accord (Acts 2:1,46). They had one mind and heart. Unity commands the blessing from God. God's call to wholeness and unity will be heeded by His standard bearers who desire the Giver more than the gifts and the Servant more than being served.

Listen to God's call to wholeness and the blessing that accompanies the call:

> Behold, how good and how pleasant it is for brethren to dwell together in unity...
>
>   For there the Lord commanded the blessing, even life for evermore (Ps. 133:1,3).

7

Called to Win

"S he looketh forth as the morning." Who is *she?* She is
the church. She marches as a terrible army under the
banner of Christ. Her call is not to invade the world
for the purpose of losing, retreating or hiding in the desert
places. She is called to overcome; to defeat the enemy; to
bring repentance, refreshing and restoration; and to win the
lost to Jesus Christ!

A family in our church came to me with their baby in
their arms during an evening service. They came forth out
of a night of tears, sorrow, weeping and depression. Tired
of being on the defensive, they took the offensive. Weary
of being overcome, they marched into the joy of the morning with faith and hope as overcomers. That's what we are
as standard bearers — *overcomers in Christ Jesus!*

"Pastor, we have the greatest need in our lives," they confessed. "We will not be satisfied until our baby gets better. We will not accept that he should die peaceably. We want to see him healed and whole. We don't want anything less than for our son to have a fully developed, completely healed and functioning brain. That is what we want and nothing less."

Were they asking too much? Had they marched too far? Were they becoming too radical in their faith? Could it be that they were raising the standard too high?

Can true sons or daughters of the Father God ask Him for what they need? Absolutely! Read the promise of Jesus:

> Ask, and it shall be given you; seek, and ye shall find; knock, and it shall be opened unto you: For every one that asketh receiveth; and he that seeketh findeth; and to him that knocketh it shall be opened. Or what man is there of you, whom if his son ask bread, will he give him a stone? Or if he ask a fish, will he give him a serpent? If ye then, being evil, know how to give good gifts unto your children, how much more shall your Father which is in heaven give good things to them that ask him? (Matt. 7:7-11).

These parents looked forth into morning. They turned their back on the night. They walked away from doubt, unbelief and negative naysayers who gave them no hope. They changed their minds from what the world said to what God said. They said, "We are depending on God to go out to the edge with us and rebuke the brain stealer. We prayed and sought God." By the stripes of Jesus, there is healing (1 Pet. 2:24).

The early church believed that and witnessed mighty healings and miracles. Faithful saints throughout the ages believed God and were healed. Wigglesworth and Sumrall have been used by God to pass this anointing on to our generation. They believed in and witnessed the healing power of God. The time has come for our generation to raise high the standard of living in a constant season of healing. We believed God for the healing of this baby, Cody.

Three months later the parents brought Cody back to the altar at church. I didn't recognize him. His head was the normal size. His parents showed me a report and other documentation that demonstrated clearly that their son had a fully developed brain.

We are she "who looketh forth as the morning...terrible as an army with banners." We have been called to overcome, to win back what the enemy has stolen. He had stolen Cody's brain. Like Brother Sumrall, we didn't just rebuke the devil, we demanded, "Put it back!" We overcame by the power of the blood and the word of our testimony (Rev. 12:11). Under the banner of Christ, we are all conquerors through Him who loved us and gave Himself for us.

To win the peace, we must enter the conflict. How does she, the church, God's army, respond to the call to win? We must understand what true peace is and how to use the weapons Christ gives us.

How Do We Win the Peace?

You can declare peace, but until the enemy is completely overcome, you have only a standoff. In recent history we've termed such a standoff, a "cold war." A cold war is still a war.

David walked into such a standoff in the valley of Elah (see 1 Sam. 17). Two armies lined up facing each other, ready for war. The battle's victory was yet to be claimed. In eternity, God had already won the battle. But a standard bearer, a David, a man of God, had to confront the enemy and claim the victory. So David proclaimed, "This day will the Lord deliver thee into mine hand; and I will smite thee, and take thine head from thee...And all this assembly shall know that the Lord saveth not with sword and spear: for the battle is the Lord's, and he will give you into our hands" (1 Sam. 17:46-47).

The battle belongs to the Lord. He has already won our peace on the cross. He has already sent the clouds saturated with blessing to shower upon us. But God needs standard bearers who will take His banner into battle and claim the victory for their lives, their families, their churches and their nations. We cannot stand by idly watching the enemy threaten and instill fear in people. The devil wins all standoffs! We've not been called to sit on the sidelines and watch while he destroys our children, our marriages, our churches and our cities. The Bible calls God's standard bearers to arm themselves:

> Put on the whole armour of God, that ye may be able to stand against the wiles of the devil. For we wrestle not against flesh and blood, but against principalities, against powers, against the rulers of the darkness of this world, against spiritual wickedness in high places. Wherefore take unto you the whole armour of God, that ye may be able to withstand in the evil day, and having done all, to stand.
>
> Stand therefore, having your loins girt about with truth, and having on the breastplate of righteousness; and your feet shod with the preparation of the gospel of peace; Above all, taking the shield of faith, wherewith ye shall be able to quench all the fiery darts of the wicked. And take the helmet of salvation, and the sword of the Spirit, which is the word of God: Praying always with all prayer and supplication in the Spirit, and watching thereunto with all persever-

ance and supplication for all saints (Eph. 6:11-18).

The Word of God is the weapon we use to bring peace. We learn it, know it, use it as a sharp, two-edged sword and overcome the enemy with it.

The Law of First Mention.

The first thing that we should learn as standard bearers in heeding our call to win is how to discern the times. The Word of God reveals to us the times in which we live. The Bible reveals that "to every thing there is a season, and a time to every purpose under the heaven...a time of war, and a time of peace" (Eccl. 3:1,8).

Our problem in today's church is that we don't understand the law of first mention in the Bible. That law simply is this: Whatever comes first in the text, comes forth first in time: that is, it happens first. Therefore, in Ecclesiastes 3, we understand that first will come a time of war and then a time of peace.

We would rather have peace without war. We want everything to be nice. We want to avoid fiery furnaces and persecution. We desire to circumvent the battle and win peace without conflict. We settle for a small puddle of God's revival in our wilderness instead of allowing Him to flood our lives with His presence. Remember, peace is not the absence of conflict. In fact, inner peace with God will bring us into confrontation with the principalities of this world.

We don't want to be thrown into the furnace. We want God to kill the king! But Shadrach, Meshach and Abednego went into the fire and there experienced the victory of the Word of God.

How often have I heard pastors and other Christians ask, "Why did God allow this [fire, trial or persecution] to happen to me?" In fact, we should count ourselves blessed that God would allow us to walk though the fire so that we could experience His victory and then give glory to His name for it.

We Must Learn How to Fight

I want you to understand that we will have a season of war before a season of peace. We are a terrible army with banners, raising high the standard, invading enemy territory and winning the peace in the name of Christ. We are in the battle. We face the Goliaths and the spiritual Saddam Husseins and drive them out of our Kuwaits, our homes, our streets and our towns. We say to every evil principality and power, "This is the season for war. Devil, I'm not just drawing a line in the sand; I am storming the beach!"

We are not fighting alone; God is always with us. He is in the desert trenches right beside us. The land may be dry and parched, with not a cloud in the desert's sky, but He promised no dry season. In the middle of the battle a downpour is going to fall and drown our adversary!

Some may protest, "But, Brother Rod, I just want to put on my designer dress or suit, find my Bible on Saturday night and come to church on Sunday morning. I want to sing three fast songs and two slow ones, take out three crumpled-up dollar bills for the offering, and raise only one hand in praise because I'm too tired to raise both hands."

It's time for war. The time for talk is over! All our discussions and rhetoric have reached the apex of their ability to inspire us and change our situations. We don't come to the table to negotiate with the enemy. We come to a table of victory spread before the enemy by our God. It's time to raise the standard, put the enemy to flight and heed God's call to win.

Yes, the millennium is coming. In the twinkling of an eye, the King will ride. Jesus will span the expanse of eternity and time. He will ride on a white stallion, cracking a whip that will sound like a thousand cannons. The Lion of Judah, the King of kings and Lord of lords, the Word of God will usher in the kingdom of God and throw Satan into the pit of hell, bound for a thousand years.

But wait, there is a problem. We're not there yet. The millennium has not yet arrived. The Bible says that in that day the lion shall lie down with the lamb. Here's a millennium test. Take a lion. Don't feed it for a week and put a lamb in its cage. If the lion lays down with the lamb, then the millennium is here. If the lion devours the lamb, the millennium is not yet here. Jesus is coming, but until He rides we are still the standard bearers invading the enemy's territory under His banner.

God is calling His church to win. His call takes us to a level beyond the status quo, beyond normalcy. We've stood on the sidelines too long, tolerating a society where right is wrong and righteousness is regarded as abnormal.

The devil does have an inner circle of darkened hearts to whom he has imparted the mystery of iniquity and the depths of degradation. Over a period of time, these doctors of damnation have worked like leaven, permeating the mind-set of the body of Christ to the point that now, not only in society but also in the church, we call evil, good, and good, evil.

Here's an example of what I mean. We live in a society that preserves the whale, the spotted owl and the whooping crane from extinction while murdering its babies in the womb and abusing its children. We have the technology to build houses strong enough to resist the ravages of hurricanes, but we cannot protect the dwelling in those homes from divorce, violent crime and addictions. We can conquer space but not our own sin habits.

All of this onslaught of evil is too subtle and too sinister to be of human design. It must be the carefully calculated conspiracy of demonic spirits. Our children come under attack daily in their schools. Guns are carried by children into elementary schools. Teachers are attacked and murdered. Teenagers are taught to practice safe sex instead of being taught abstinence.

> There's only one thing that our enemy understands: somebody with a bigger stick than his.

We excuse sin in America with euphemisms. Immorality is called simply an "alternative lifestyle." Liars are merely extroverts with lively imaginations. Alcoholics are seen not as addicts but as victims of society. Murderers are now called the unfortunate victims of their environment. Our society tries to justify a son's killing of his parents by claiming that he is emotionally damaged and abused. Children now can divorce their parents.

The demons are on the attack. The devil has one thought in mind: to steal, kill and destroy (John 10:10).

There's only one thing that our enemy understands: somebody with a bigger stick than his. Listen to God's promise to us whom He has called to win: "Greater is he that is in you, than he that is in the world" (1 John 4:4).

Let me give you an analogy. Remember our nation's battle strategy in Vietnam? We fought a war of containment. We tried to maintain a standoff with the enemy. I'll never forget the television reports showing our men on top of the U.S. embassy in Saigon climbing like animals across the rooftop and being picked up by helicopter as they retreated from the enemy we tried to contain. Yes, we had dropped enough bombs on them to sink the whole country into the China Sea. We had broadcast propaganda for years against the communists. But we had not fought to win, and so, we lost.

The Gulf War was in contrast to the situation in Vietnam. Iraq invaded Kuwait on August 2, 1990. Shortly thereafter President George Bush sent forces to oust the illegal invaders of Iraq from Kuwaiti soil. Banners were raised. Flags were flown. A nation prayed. Mamas started baking apple pies. Fighting men were saluted as they left to report to National Guard bases. Our Commander-in-Chief gave an ultimatum to Iraq that its troops must leave before January 15, 1991, or they would be pushed out by force. General "Stormin' Norman" Schwartzkopf prepared to kick the invaders all the way back to Baghdad. American patriotism skyrocketed. We were in Desert Storm not just to hold the line but to win, and win we did.

It's time for war. It's time to get in the devil's face and let him know that his invasion of your mind, your body, your emotions, your finances and your church will not be tolerated. Not only will you resist him, but you will also overcome him by the Word of God and drive him back by the blood of the Lamb.

> It's time for war. It's time to get in the devil's face and let him know that his invasion of your mind, your body, your emotions, your finances and your church will not be tolerated.

When Will God's Standard Bearers Be Ready to Fight?

Nobody likes a fight, but in this matter we have no choice. In reference to the war against Vietnam, strategists are still trying to figure out what we were doing. In Operation Desert Storm, we knew exactly what we were doing. President George Bush said, "Enemy invaders of Kuwait, you must go voluntarily, or you will go by force. The American people read of the atrocities committed by the Iraqi soldiers in Kuwait, and we are ready to fight."

I wonder, what will it take for the church to stand up, draw a line in the sand and fight for something more than spiritual mirages lacking any ounce of living water to quench her thirst? When will God's standard bearers climb out of their spiritual playpens, strap on their helmets of salvation, load up the bayonets of God's Word and say, "It's time to go to war"? How many atrocities committed by the devil and his demons will it take before we are ready to fight?

How many more crack babies have to be born? How many more church families must be broken up by divorce? How many more church kids must be lured into cults? How many more aborted children must be piled up in trash cans and thrown into incinerators? How many more families will have to stand at a casket weeping for a loved one killed by a drunken driver or a drug overdose? What will it take for us to rise up in righteous indignation, leave the flatlands of dry spiritual existence and move into a deluge of the Spirit of God?

How many more preachers do we have to watch fall from grace until somebody says, "No more. It's time for war"? How many more dead church services and empty altars will there be? How long will we continue to run after this man and that blessing while a hurting, depressed, destitute world remains lost and dying without God?

The gates of hell cannot prevail against the church who refuses to live in dry wastelands but rightfully pursues and possesses all that belongs to her.

The church is called to wholeness. As a unified body, we cannot only face the enemy, we can heed the call to win, defeating the enemy where we find him. In these final days before Jesus' return, it doesn't matter what your skin color is or what your denominational background or social class may be. We are pulling down the walls that divide us, and as one in Christ we are coming against a common enemy. He is the devil, and we will fight until we win!

My wife, daughter and I were invited to a meeting in New Orleans at the Louisiana Superdome. We were the only whites there. Forty thousand African American Christians had invited me there to preach the gospel. I told them, "You all are black by birth. I'm black by choice. Do you understand what I am saying? Lay down any barrier that stands between you and another brother or sister in Christ. We are on the same side. We're standard bearers in the same terrible, awesome army going forth under the banner of Jesus Christ."

The gates of hell cannot prevail against the church who refuses to live in dry wastelands but rightfully pursues and possesses all that belongs to her.

The Bible says it this way: "There is one body, and one Spirit, even as ye are called in one hope of your calling; One Lord, one faith, one baptism, One God and Father of all, who is above all, and through all, and in you all" (Eph. 4:4-6).

Use Your Spiritual Weapons

Now that you are a standard bearer wearing God's armor, discerning the time of war and willing to heed to call to win, what are your weapons and how will you use them? Having a cause, desiring to win, and being passion-ate for righteousness are not enough. You must become tired of the adversary's occupation in your life. You need to say, "Accusing adversary, you don't belong here, and I'm not tolerating your presence any more!" What are the weapons you must have and use?

1. Stand firm.

Suppose your attack is from depression. Say, "I'm not putting up with depression any longer." Are you willing to stand against the enemy? You've run to this preacher to be prayed for and that Christian writer to read his book's advice. You've been anointed until you look like a greased pig at a county fair, but you still have not picked up your Bible to know the weapons of your warfare.

You may have paid some crash diet program hundreds of dollars, but you cannot break the spirit of gluttony in your life, much less fast and pray for the kingdom of God.

Are you tired of leaving your weapons on the shelf? Are you ready to stand firm, take up the sword of the Spirit — God's Word — and use all the weapons Christ has given you as a standard bearer?

2. Know, meditate upon and apply the Word of God.

Your most effective weapon in answering God's call to win is the Bible. The strategy and the training for battle is found in His Word. In fact, the rifle for your battle is God's Word. In Desert Storm the soldiers told us, "We ate sand. We slept in sand. We ran in the sand. We found sand in places we didn't know had sand. They handed us a rifle. Every day it was, open it, break it apart, clean it, oil it, put it back together, load it, shoot it, prepare to use it. We had to sleep with it and eat with it. When we attacked, we were ready to use it, and we won with it."

I envision an army of God so equipped with the Word of

God that they live with it, eat with it, sleep with it and use it every moment of every day. We have the weapon. It's time to use it constantly. With three simple words from the Bible, Jesus defeated the devil in the wilderness. He said simply, "It is written" (Luke 4:4).

It is time for war. The battle is raging. The devil is telling you you will always be in the desert. But you are the standard bearer. Know and use the Word.

A soldier being interviewed in the midst of Desert Storm said that he was paralyzed with fear when he first entered a battle and started the attack. He said that his feet and arms would not move. For a moment he forgot everything he had learned. Suddenly, his hand went to the bolt action of the rifle. His training kicked in, and he went forward blazing his rifle at the enemy. He said that it seemed as if he were standing outside himself watching himself fight.

Let me warn you. The time will come when the flaming missiles of the adversary will be sailing all around you. You will not have time to reason, to think and to work through what you must do. But if you have the Word of God in you, suddenly the Holy Spirit is going to take over. The Word is the sword of the Spirit. He will put words in your mouth when you don't know what to say (Luke 21:15). God's Spirit in you will blaze forth, devastating the enemy with the Word.

The apostles Peter and John walked up to the Gate Beautiful. A begging, lame man said, "I need something." The apostles didn't say, "Next week, we're having special services at our church. We will go there and get prayed up. We need to hear that healing evangelist and get a word from him. Then we'll talk to you." No! Peter declared, "Silver and gold have I none; but such as I have give I thee: In the name of Jesus Christ of Nazareth rise up and walk" (Acts 3:6).

The apostles were standing firm in Christ. They knew the

living Word. They spoke the Word, and the enemy was defeated. Peter took the lame man by the right hand and lifted him up, and the Holy Spirit came all over them. The lame man was healed. The enemy was defeated by the blood of the Lamb and the word of their testimony.

3. After standing firm and taking up the sword of the Spirit — God's Word — then pray.

How much and how often should you pray? "Pray without ceasing" (1 Thess. 5:17). In Ephesians 6:18, Paul identifies the "all's" of prayer. Standard bearers are to pray always with *all* prayer and supplication with *all* perseverance for *all* saints. When you get up in the morning, pray. When you go to bed, pray. When you're driving your car, pray with your eyes open. When you're tired of praying, pray some more. Close yourself in your closet and pray. Grab your spouse and pray. Leave the family sleeping in bed. Get up in the middle of the night and pray. Stop talking about prayer, reading books about prayer and going to seminars to learn to pray. Start doing it — pray!

4. Go to church.

Every time the doors open, be there. Be in the worship services. Pray, fellowship and study in the home groups and the Bible classes. Be there for mid-week services, prayer meetings and camp meetings. "Not forsaking the assembling of ourselves together, as the manner of some is; but exhorting one another: and so much the more, as ye see the day approaching" (Heb. 10:25).

5. Witness your faith.

Having a supply line for the troops is so important in battle. Faith is part of our supply line in the church. The testimony of the faith of others builds up my faith. Your healing encourages me to pray for my healing and the healing of others in the body of Christ. Sharing with me about your miracles builds my faith to trust God for my miracles. Don't keep your prayers to yourself. Pray for others in faith. The prayer of a righteous standard bearer will avail much in God's army. Build others up in the Lord.

Satan is defeated by the blood of the Lamb and the word of our testimony (Rev. 12:11). Listen to Paul's encouragement in 1 Thessalonians 5:14-15, "Gently encourage the stragglers, and reach out for the exhausted, pulling them to their feet. Be patient with each person, attentive to individual needs. And be careful that when you get on each other's nerves you don't snap at each other. Look for the best in each other, and always do your best to bring it out" (*The Message*). Encouraging other standard bearers is a mighty witness to your faith in Christ.

6. Guard your heart.

Set armed guards around your mind and your emotions. Guard your eyes and ears. Be careful what you watch on television or listen to on the radio. Don't bring an immoral video, book or magazine into your home. Stay away from anything that would pollute your mind. Remember: To permit is to participate. You may not commit adultery, murder or steal, but if you allow sinful behavior into your house through different forms of so-called entertainment, it is the same as if you were committing the very act yourself.

Guard your heart. "Be careful [anxious] for nothing; but in every thing by prayer and supplication with thanksgiving let your requests be made known unto God. And the peace of God, which passeth all understanding, shall keep [guard] your hearts and minds through Christ Jesus" (Phil. 4:6-7).

7. Praise God.

In Desert Storm we counterattacked the Scud missiles of Iraq with our Patriot missiles. The incoming invader was met with an outgoing attack. Praising God for the promises that we trust Him to perform puts the enemy on the defensive and drives him from the land. Praise God for what you know He will do based in His promises. His Word will not return void. Speak His promises. Declare His praise.

God asked Jeremiah, "What seest thou?" Jeremiah answered, "I see a rod of an almond tree" (Jer. 1:11). Then God said, "Thou hast well seen: for I will hasten my word to perform it" (v. 12). There were no almonds on the tree. Only the bud could be seen. Yet God confirmed that His Word would be performed. Look at the almond tree in the winter or early spring. There is no fruit yet, but the promise of fruit is in the tree.

The same is true in the life of a standard bearer. You may be in the midst of winter, but you can trust and praise God for the coming fruit of His promises. His Word of promise has been planted and hidden in your heart. His promises are spoken by your lips and lifted in praise.

Anybody can offer God the sacrifice of praise on a clear day in the midst of a season of plenty (Heb. 13:15). Anyone can sing a tune in the noonday sun. But God gives His people, His standard bearers, a song to sing at midnight when trouble is closing in and darkness surrounds. Defeat the enemy with a shout of praise.

Don't clap your hands in worship because everyone is clapping or the music is upbeat. We are a kingdom of priests called to clap our hands in praise of almighty God. "O clap your hands, all ye people; shout unto God with the voice of triumph" (Ps. 47:1). There is victory in praise.

The Bible says that we are to lift up holy hands in praise of God (Ps. 63:4; 134:2; Lam. 3:41; 1 Tim. 2:8). Put the enemy on the defensive with an outgoing attack of praise. Have you see in sports what uplifted hands mean? It signifies scoring, making an offensive goal and winning. Lift up your hands in worship and praise. You have heeded the call to win, and you are more than a conqueror in Christ Jesus.

8.   Pray in the Spirit.

Romans 8:26 reminds us that "We know not what we should pray for as we ought: but the Spirit itself maketh intercession for us with groanings which cannot be uttered." When I think of warfare and praying in the Spirit, the picture of a stealth bomber comes to mind. In Desert Storm the stealth bomber looked like a big, black stingray. It flew hundreds of sorties and never even got a scratch from the enemy. Do you know why? Enemy radar could not detect it.

The same is true of praying in the Spirit. When we pray in tongues we slip right by the enemy, through enemy-held territory, and the devil doesn't know a thing. We won the Gulf War with air superiority. Praying in the Spirit gives us spiritual superiority over the enemy. He cannot touch us.

9.   Be confident in the Lord.

Finally, in the Gulf War we had great confidence in our Commander-in-Chief, President Bush. From General Norman Schwartzkopf to the lowest-ranking soldier to the citizen on the street, we Americans believed that the commander had a winning strategy.

Far exceeding the plans of any human commander are the plans of the King of kings and Lord of lords. He has a winning strategy and more. He has already won through His death and resurrection. Our risen Lord declared, "All power is given unto me in heaven and earth. Go ye therefore, and teach all nations, baptizing them in the name of the Father, and of the Son, and of the Holy Ghost: Teaching them to observe all things whatsoever I have commanded you: and, lo, I am with you always, even unto the end of the world" (Matt. 28:18-20). You can have confidence in the delegated authority and power of Jesus. When He sends us, we go with power.

Heed the call to win. Be confident. "For we are made partakers of Christ, if we hold the beginning of our confidence stedfast unto the end" (Heb. 3:14). We win because the enemy has already been defeated at the cross. We win because as we go forth into the morning, fair as the moon and clear as the sun, we, terrible as an army, march under Christ's banner raising high His standard.

Not only are we called to wholeness and called to win, but we are also called to worship. The mighty Warrior who leads us deserves all honor, glory, worship and praise. Let's turn now to the call to worship.

8

Called to Worship

On Father's Day a few years ago our church received a divine mandate to heed the call to worship. In years past some from our church had gone to the homosexual parade in our city held each Father's Day. Normally, we would pray in the Holy Spirit along the sidewalk as the parade passed by. When we were finished, we thought we had done battle with the enemy, but little had happened.

But on this particular Father's Day I shared with our church, "I'll tell you what we need to do at the parade today. We need to go there and not talk to anyone but God. We shouldn't talk to God about what we want Him to do. Rather, we should praise Him. We should thank Him. These people need to know of the love of Jesus, so while they

> God inhabits our praises. And when He shows up, healing, deliverance, salvation and miracles begin to manifest.

walk through the middle of us, let's just stand still and lift our hands in praise to God."

A young boy who was clinically deaf in both ears was worshiping with our congregation that day. Although several people including myself had prayed with him prior to that day for his healing, he still remained deaf. On this day he went to the parade to worship and praise God.

Standing on the streets of Columbus, Ohio, the saints — the standard bearers — of the most high God began to focus on Him. We glorified, praised, adored, thanked and worshiped God all along that parade route. Suddenly, the young boy was completely healed! In the midst of worship and praise, God miraculously unstopped his ears.

Why? Just as in the days of Jehoshaphat, when God's people worship and praise Him, He sets an ambush for the enemy. God inhabits our praises. And when He shows up, healing, deliverance, salvation and miracles begin to manifest.

What kind of standard bearers is God seeking? In John 4, Jesus talks with a Samaritan woman about worship. A void filled her life. She was parched from the lack of the fresh rain of worship in her life. She had been married five times and now lived with a man who was not her husband. Jesus revealed the truth about her life to her and invited her to become a vessel of true worship out of which His living water would flow. Jesus said:

> But the hour cometh, and now is, when the true
> worshippers shall worship the Father in spirit and in

truth: for the Father seeketh such to worship him.
God is a Spirit: and they that worship him must
worship him in spirit and in truth (John 4:23-24).

God is seeking those who will worship Him in spirit and
in truth.

What is true worship? Second Chronicles 20 tells a powerful story about true worship. The enemies of Judah — the
children of Ammon and Moab — came to attack with a
huge army (v. 1). Jehoshaphat, king of Judah, cried out
to God, "What shall we do?" The king and all of Judah,
adults and children alike, stood before God seeking His
protection (vv. 12-13). In summary, God replied, "Don't
worry about it. Just stand firm praising and worshiping
Me. When you go out into battle in the morning, you
won't have to fight. For the battle is not yours. You just
stand still. Stand still and praise me. When you glorify Me
and I receive the sacrifice of your praise, I will be there!
I will manifest My presence, and your adversaries will be
destroyed" (vv. 15-17).

Look at what happened when Judah worshiped the Lord:

> And when he [Jehoshaphat] had consulted with
> the people, he appointed singers unto the Lord,
> and that should praise the beauty of holiness, as
> they went out before the army, and to say, Praise
> the Lord; for his mercy endureth forever. And
> when they began to sing and to praise, the Lord
> set ambushments against the children of Ammon,
> Moab, and mount Seir, who were come against
> Judah; and they were smitten (2 Chron. 20:21-22).

Do you realize how little we know about worship in
the church? Yet over one-third of the book of Hebrews is
devoted to worship. One-third of the Old Testament talks
about worship. The longest book of the Bible is a book of

songs for worship. Yet the body of Christ has been so impotent in responding to the call to worship. If you want to be a power-filled standard bearer for Christ, then heed the call to worship!

"She looked forth as the morning, fair as the moon, clear as the sun, terrible as an army with banners" (Song 6:10). She — you and me, the church — must heed the calls of Christ to wholeness to win at war and to worship. At the core of a standard bearer's life is worship. Worship brings us into the refreshing presence of God, and our barren spirits become inundated with the spring rains. No change ever happens outside of His presence. Without the presence of God in a man, a church, an institution or a television broadcast, we can never be changed.

We come into His presence through thanksgiving, praise and worship. Psalm 22:3 declares that God inhabits the praises of His people. First Peter 2:9 describes the church of Jesus Christ as a people of praise: "But ye are a chosen generation, a royal priesthood, an holy nation, a peculiar people; that ye should show forth the praises of him who hath called you out of darkness into his marvellous light." The chief end of man is to glorify, to worship and to praise God. Jesus asserted, "Thou shalt worship the Lord thy God, and him only shalt thou serve" (Matt. 4:10).

How do we truly worship God? I want to demonstrate to you the meaning of worship hidden in the Old Testament ark of the covenant. Walk with me from the outer court of thanksgiving to the inner court of praise and into the holy of holies to worship God in spirit and in truth.

The Ark and Worship

In Exodus God commanded the people of Israel to build the furnishings and the vessels for worship. He started with instructions on building the ark of the covenant in Exodus 25:10-21. After giving His detailed instructions on how to build the ark, God commanded, "And thou shalt put the mercy seat above upon the ark; and in the ark thou shalt put the testimony that I shall give thee. And there I will meet with thee" (Ex. 25:21-22).

But wait. There is no tabernacle yet. There is no holy of holies. God is having them build an ark to go into a dwelling place that has yet to be constructed. God is giving the children of Israel the blueprint whereby He will allow them to approach His presence. God was not giving them something or doing something for them. The focus here is not the ark but the place of meeting. God wants His people to meet with Him, to come into His presence. The tabernacle for worship eventually contained many different pieces of furniture and vessels for worship. But the first object built was the ark.

Notice the principle of worship established here. God told the Israelites, "Don't build the outer court first. Don't construct the altar of sacrifice, the table of shewbread or the candlestick first. Don't build the altar of incense first. Build the ark of the covenant first." Why? This is where the shekinah glory of God resides. This is where the anointing is housed. This is where we come into His presence. He was saying, "You must first find me, and then you build everything else around me." Worship begins in the presence of God.

The ark represents God's presence in our lives. It was built of wood. This represents the humanity of Jesus, the Son of Man. He was not deity humanized or humanity deified. He was the perfect God-Man. The wood of the ark was overlaid with gold. This represents divinity, the deity of Jesus Christ, the Son of God. The staves that carried the ark symbolize to us that God wants to go wherever we go. God promised, "I will never leave you nor forsake you" (see Deut. 31:6).

When you walk through the valley, the ark goes with

you. God is there. Worship Him in the valley. When you climb a mountain, God goes with you. Worship Him on the mountain. When you go into battle, the ark goes before you. Worship Him in the battle. The battle belongs to the Lord. He goes before you to vanquish your enemies. Everything centers around the ark.

Let's examine certain things that God put inside the ark.

1.   Aaron's rod that budded was placed in the ark.

This represented the resurrection power of God. Take the ark, take your worship of God into your dead marriage — it can live again. If your finances are dead, take the ark there. Worship God. Your finances can be resurrected. Your relationships, your joy, your sick body, all things can be raised to new life when you come into His presence with thanksgiving, praise and worship.

2.   The tablets of the law were put inside of the ark.

God gave Moses the decalogue, or Ten Commandments, and He prepared a place for that Word. Have you deposited the Word into the center of your worship and praise? God wants to get into your situation, but you need to make room for Him in your heart. We speak, we sing, we pray and we declare God's Word in true worship.

3.   Manna was placed in the ark.

This represented God's sustenance. Jesus said, "I am the bread of life: he that cometh to me shall never hunger; and he that believeth on me shall never thirst...I am that bread of life. Your fathers did eat manna in the wilderness, and are dead. This is the bread which cometh down from heaven, that a man may eat thereof, and not die. I am the living bread which came down from heaven: if any man eat of this bread, he shall live forever: and the bread that I will give is my flesh, which I will give for the life of the world" (John 6:35, 48-51).

It doesn't matter if you are in the wilderness and all of your friends have forsaken you. It doesn't matter who likes you or how much money you have in the bank. Before God will let you starve, He will open up the heavens and rain down manna from His supply. He desires to be your sole Source of supply for every need. In worship we partake of living bread and there find life.

4. Across the mercy seat of the ark were the cherubim with their wings outstretched.

They sit there and gaze at the mercy seat. Why? Angels never knew the joy of a standard bearer. They never knew our joy at having our sins washed away by the blood of Christ. Though they sing in heaven, they will never be able to sing the standard bearer's song, "Oh! precious is the flow that makes me white as snow; no other fount I know, nothing but the blood of Jesus."

What does that mercy seat sprinkled with the blood of Jesus represent for God's church who looketh forth as the morning? It represents the night that should have come but never did because of the mercy of God. It represents all the *should haves, could haves* and *might haves.* It represents every car that should have hit you but never did because of God's mercy. That mercy seat represents every disease that should have afflicted you or your family but never did because of the blood of Christ. Just as it did during the Exodus, the blood causes death, destruction and devastation to pass over God's people.

For the church that worships, the snare that the enemy has laid must pass over. The destruction that lays waste at noonday is going to see the blood of Jesus and have to pass over. God desires that true worshipers come into the holy of holies and there meet everything that the ark represents — the presence of the living God. How do we get to the ark of worship?

Dr. Lester Sumrall imparted to me the great revelation that man is a spirit, possesses a soul and lives in a body. As I began to study God's Word I noticed that God seems to do everything in threes: the trinity — Father, Son and Holy Spirit; the three archangels — Michael, Gabriel and Lucifer; man — spirit, soul and body. It is therefore easy to draw the analogy of thanksgiving, praise and worship as a progression from the outer court to the inner court to the holy of holies. Our journey begins first with thanksgiving.

The Outer Court of Thanksgiving

With our bodies, our physical beings, we come into the outer court with thanksgiving. Seven times a year Israel would climb up to the temple mount singing the psalms of ascent, "Enter into his gates with thanksgiving, and into his courts with praise: be thankful unto him, and bless his name" (Ps. 100:4).

The outer court of the tabernacle was illuminated by natural light. Psalm 150:6 says, "Let every thing that hath breath praise the Lord." This is a natural response. Thanksgiving is natural. Anyone can do it. Worship begins with thanksgiving. This is where you rehearse those things you can see with natural light.

There are several expressions of thanksgiving. When we thank God we clap our hands. We lift our hands and shout with a voice of triumph. We dance before the Lord. The Bible says that when David recovered the ark from the house of his friend Obed-Edom he went toward the city with gladness. But after six steps he came to the end of himself. For when he went to take the next step something overcame him and he "danced before the Lord with all his might" (2 Sam. 6:14).

We use our bodies to express thanksgiving to the Lord because we have His glory, and we are not bound to the beggarly elements of this natural world! We are thankful for what we can see: our salvation, healing deliverance, our families, our churches, our jobs, God's abundant provision in our lives. He is alive and all around us!

Giving thanks means counting our blessings. I was told the story of a man who owned a small estate and wished to sell it. He contacted a real estate agent and asked the agent to write an ad for the house and place it in the newspaper.

When the ad was ready, the agent took it to the owner for approval before he printed it.

The man read it over. The real estate agent slid the contract to list the house on the market across the table for him to sign, but he said, "I can't sign this."

The agent said, "Why not? You called me here. I have written the ad. I thought you wanted to sell your house."

He said, "Well, I did, but when I started reading what you said about my place, I realized I have been looking for a place like that for years!"

We need to be more thankful. Count your blessings. Start thanking God by asking Him to open your eyes to see what you already have in Christ Jesus. Have an attitude of gratitude. Thank God for all He has done in your life.

Remember when God brought the children of Israel out of Egyptian slavery? God could not take them into the promised land because they were not thankful for being brought out of bondage (see Ex. 16). Before I allow a person to complain in my presence, I often ask him to tell me ten things he is thankful for. By the time he has finished thanking God, he has forgotten why he was complaining!

Unlike the Egyptians, David rehearsed his victories to Saul and said, "The Lord that delivered me out of the paw of the lion, and out of the paw of the bear, he will deliver me out of the hand of this Philistine" (1 Sam. 17:37). Thank

God for what he has already done for you — health in your body, your paid bills. Continually offer up the sacrifice of praise.

The Inner Court of Praise

Once we thank the Lord with our physical beings, then we move into the inner court to praise Him with our souls. This holy place was not illuminated with natural light but with golden candlesticks which represent the light of the Word of God. When you have a word from God, you have a memorial, a place of remembrance to go when doubt and trouble close in.

A word from the Lord can come in two ways: as a prophetic word or as a word from Scripture. I remember almost twenty years ago when our church had about 150 people in it, God gave me a prophetic word. In my mind I thought it would be a good idea to do a fifteen-minute radio broadcast. But the Lord spoke to me to go on television. That concept staggered me. How could we possibly go on television? We were a young church with a lot of vision but not much money.

Of course, we were in need of equipment, and I had my mind set on some television cameras which were not very expensive. The Lord spoke again and said, "I am going to give you two Ikegami ITC 350 cameras." At the time, these cameras were way beyond our financial means.

But this word exploded in my spirit so much that I would have the congregation turn and face where those cameras should be and begin to praise and and believe God for them. They were more real to me than if they were already there. We would spend long seasons of rejoicing and confession over those cameras. I had flyers printed and distributed to the congregation to take home and to work to praise God for our new cameras.

As He promised, our need was supplied, and today we

are broadcasting our *Breakthrough* television program to 14,000 stations and cable affiliates and 136 nations of the world!

As I mentioned, the second way God's word comes to us is through Scripture. Mark 11:22-24 says, "And Jesus answering saith unto them, Have faith in God. For verily I say unto you, That whosoever *shall* say unto this mountain, Be thou removed, and be thou cast into the sea; and *shall* not doubt in his heart, but *shall* believe that those things which he saith *shall* come to pass; he *shall* have whatsoever he saith. Therefore I say unto you, What things soever ye desire, when ye pray, believe that ye receive them, and ye *shall* have them" (italics added).

In other words, your healing may not have come yet, but you have God's Word on it and you *shall* have it. Your loved ones may still be lost, but they *shall* be saved. We do not serve a halfway God who sometimes answers prayer. God's Word transcends time and space, and whatsoever He has said unto you, you *shall* have it. He will cause the former and latter rain to come together in the same month, and you will have no dry season!

Jeremiah saw a vision of an almond tree blossoming and bearing fruit in the middle of winter (see Jer. 1:11). What a sight that must have been! Trees do not bear fruit in the dead of winter with four feet of snow on the ground and the temperature below freezing. But God says, "When you offer the fruit of your lips to Me, right in the middle of your situation I will cause life to spring forth, and you will have that which I have promised!"

God said of His Word, "As the rain cometh down, and the snow from heaven, and returneth not thither, but watereth the earth, and maketh it bring forth and bud, that it may give seed to the sower, and bread to the eater: So shall my word be that goeth forth out of my mouth: it shall not return unto me void, but it shall accomplish that which

I please, and it shall prosper in the thing whereto I sent it" (Is. 55:10-11).

Look at what this verse means. God said He sends His word down to earth, but it is our responsibility to return it to Him in praise. Hebrews 13:15 tells us we are to "offer the sacrifice of praise to God continually, that is, the fruit of our lips giving thanks to his name." Just having a word from God is not enough. We are to offer it back to Him as an expression of our faith. But when God's words go back to Him, He says, "Yes, I agree with that," and so He hastens to perform His word.

God wants us to praise Him in every situation. We sang praises to God while the homosexuals paraded down our city streets. God inhabited our praises and healing came. Paul and Silas sang praises at midnight while in jail and suddenly an earthquake opened the prison doors and broke the shackles that bound them.

I was told the story of a couple, two Moody Bible Institute graduates, John and Elain Beekman. God called them to missionary work among the Chol Indians of southern Mexico. They rode mules and traveled by dugout canoes to reach this tribe. They labored twenty-five years with other missionaries to translate the New Testament in the Chol Indian language.

Today, more than 12,000 Christians comprise the Chol Christian community. What's interesting is that when the Beekmans came, the Chol Indians didn't know how to sing. With the coming of the gospel, however, the believers in the tribe became know as "the singers." They loved to sing now, because they had something to sing about.[2]

Paul and Silas had something to sing about even though they had been falsely accused, beaten with rods and locked in stocks in a Philippian jail (see Acts 16:25). We might ask, "Why were they so happy?" It was because their consciousness was not of prison but of God. Though they were physically bound in stocks, their souls were free to praise. Their songs were born not of burden, but of gladness.

They were God's standard bearers taking the gospel to the world. Standard bearers do not understand the meaning of a dry season because they sing praises at midnight and trust God's ways, not man's. Those who sing in prison can never truly be bound. Standard bearers who sing praises continually will never cease to fulfill their destiny. Paul and Silas's praise not only opened prison doors but also led a jailer and his family to Christ (see Acts 16:26-34). Praise changes things. And praise is the hinge upon which the door of worship swings open.

Worship in the Holy of Holies

As you enter the holy of holies in worship, you meet with God and He meets with you. When you get here it doesn't matter if you can't see the answer to your prayer or if there is not even the illumination of His Word to hang your faith upon because you have Him. It doesn't matter if you are going through the flood because you know He is with you. The fiery trials and narrow valleys are meaningless because here, in true worship, you discover:

- He is the Lily of the valley.

- He is the Honey in a rock.

- He is the Staff of life.

In the outer court you have the promise of His word, but in the holy of holies you have His presence!

W.E. Vine states that worship is defined nowhere in the Bible. Why? Because it is impossible to describe with words the presence and holiness of God. When we come into the holy of holies in worship, we commune with the living God.

One of the greatest hindrances to worship in our lives is the separation between the religious and the real. We think that religion consists of prayer, reading the Bible, worship and Christian service. Our real life, on the other hand, involves eating, sleeping, cleaning the house, working, grocery shopping and the like. In God's kingdom there is no separation. The standard bearer lifting high the standard of Christ does *everything* in life to the glory of God. "Whether therefore ye eat, or drink, or whatsoever ye do, do all to the glory of God" (1 Cor. 10:31).

> We must practice living to the glory of God so that daily labors become acts of worship. Every simple act of daily living becomes a priestly act offered to God.

What does this verse mean? If Jesus has come to tabernacle with us, He never leaves us. We can worship Him anytime, any place, no matter what else we are doing.

Paul, an apostle of Jesus Christ, was a tentmaker, but he also wrote two-thirds of the New Testament. Both his tentmaking and his writing were received by God with equal affection as worship. When my wife, Joni, does the dishes or fixes dinner, God receives her activity as an humble act of worship. God receives even our eating and sleeping as worship if we do these things unto Him.

We must practice living to the glory of God so that daily labors become acts of worship. Every simple act of daily living becomes a priestly act offered to God.

We find Him ever present to receive this offering of worship. God desires that we seek Him. "They should seek the

Lord, if haply they might feel after him, and find him, though he be not far from every one of us: For in him we live, and move, and have our being" (Acts 17:27-28).

What is worship? The Bible says, "Give unto the Lord the glory due unto his name; worship the Lord in the beauty of holiness" (Ps. 29:2). *Holiness* is the state of being separated or sanctified unto God. The "beauty of holiness" refers to the condition of fulfilling the purpose for which one has been sanctified. That is worship.

It is not worship for you to sing before thousands if God's purpose for you is to work in the nursery. How many people applaud you means absolutely nothing, but purpose means everything to God.

When our hearts and motives are pure in seeking to worship God, then the world becomes a tabernacle, and living life is the incense of worship. In true worship a standard bearer discovers the abundant life in Christ as he yields himself wholly to God and desires to fulfill God's purpose in every word and deed.

Come into the outer court, the inner court and the holy of holies every moment of your day. Remember that worship doesn't happen just because a worship service is going on in a church building. In fact, you don't need the building to worship God. You are the tent. You are the tabernacle. Within you dwells the Holy Spirit. Your heart has received the gift of the Holy Spirit.

When the Holy Spirit came to indwell you, a consuming fire purified the crucible of your heart making it an ark. The blood of Christ cleansed you of every sin, washing over your life and preparing a mercy seat for the ark of your heart. At the depths of your being is a tent, a tabernacle, a holy of holies for your worship and meeting with God. Jesus made it all possible.

"The Word became flesh and dwelt among us" (John 1:14). The word *dwelt* means "tabernacled." Jesus tabernacled among us. This is where God met with man and man met with God. Jesus Christ has become your Mediator, your meeting place with God. He has given you the Holy Spirit. Because of Christ, the holy of holies now resides in your heart. Enter in, worship and meet with God.

The standard bearer's life is a call to worship. Every moment of every day can be a time of worship. The psalmist says, "Worship the Lord in the beauty of holiness" (Ps. 29:2). As you fulfill God's calling and purpose in your life, you are worshiping Him. When a standard bearer is fulfilling the purpose of God, then all of life becomes a sanctuary dedicated to the worship of God.

Every day as you practice an awareness of God's presence, your life becomes consecrated for His purpose, and therefore everything you do is exactly what God directs you to do. Psalm 37:23 says, "The steps of a good man are ordered by the Lord: and he delighteth in his way."

One morning before going to preach at my church I got into my "buck truck." That's my hunting truck. It's not fancy; when it bounces down the road, black smoke billows out the back. That morning before driving to service I got into my buck truck and closed the door. I put my hands on the steering wheel, and a prayer came to my lips. "Lord, I sanctify this day to you. In order for me to do what you purposed for me to do, I've got to get in this truck and drive from here to there." That means that what I'm doing right now, driving this buck truck down the road, is received as the same worship as if I were standing on a platform preaching to thousands.

Suddenly, tears started streaming down my face. I realized that my being aware of the presence of God and seeking Him made me feel as if He were right there beside me. I prayed, "God, you're receiving this humble act of worship. You are in my life. I'm conscious that you are here, and it makes me want to praise you and thank you. It makes me aware that no matter what I'm doing or going through, you have built your tent with me."

No longer do thanksgiving, praise or worship require effort. Worship flows out of my inner being like a river of living water. My life is worship unto Him. I pray that as a standard bearer your whole life will reflect His call to worship.

This is my vision for you: not that you will find God, but that you will recognize Him. He is all around you. He will heal you when you are washing dishes. He will deliver you when you are driving down the road.

Let your life become the tent of meeting in which God dwells and is worshiped in spirit and truth, and allow His presence to permeate your life.

Conclusion

A Call to Warning

From Adam to Noah, Abraham to Joseph, Moses to Joshua, David to Solomon, Elijah to Elisha, Isaiah to Malachi, John the Baptist to Peter, Paul to St. Augustine, Luther to Wesley, Wigglesworth to Sumrall, God has used standard bearers in every generation to raise high the standard of Jesus Christ.

We are the final generation lifting high the standard today. We are destined for the experiential, manifestation of the glory of God; destined to experience a perpetual rain and harvest in our lives; *destined for no dry seasons!*

The church is she who looks forth from the darkness into the morning. Fair as the moon, we reflect the glory of the Son. Clear as the sun, we are transparent before God — repentant, refreshed and restored to new life and awaiting the Bridegroom's return. Terrible as an army with banners we invade our world, proclaiming the gospel of Christ; taking back everything the enemy has stolen; planting His banners throughout the land; and declaring that the kingdom of heaven is at hand.

God is raising up standard bearers who sound the warning: Jesus Christ is coming soon! Repent! Be refreshed through the wind, rain, fire and power of the Holy Spirit. Restore to the kingdom what has been lost.

Terrible as an army God's people must now raise the standard and fly the banners of Christ over their lives, families, churches and nation. Time is short. Today is the day of salvation. The Lord comes as a thief in the night. The blossom on the fig tree — Israel — is in full

> Jesus Christ is coming soon! Repent! Be refreshed through the wind, rain, fire and power of the Holy Spirit. Restore to the kingdom what has been lost.

bloom. The signs of the times have started the countdown to the rapture of the church. Heavenly hosts and clouds of witnesses are watching, peering over heaven's sapphire sill to catch a glimpse of the bride — without stain or blemish — who is preparing to meet the Bridegroom.

We are speeding through critical intersections, ignoring the flashing warning lights that tell us our culture is self-destructing while our churches withdraw into their ivory tower fortresses, believing that defense is the best strategy.

God calls us to look forth as the morning, not to hide in the night. He calls us to shine and put our blazing banner high upon a hill, not hide it as an ember within the confines of our own hearts. He commissions us, His terrible army with banners, to go into all the world and not to retreat behind stained glass windows.

Heed the warning call of God. Raise the standard. Lift high the banners of Christ. Be a holy, mighty, terrible army of standard bearers ready to claim this final generation for the kingdom of God.

It's time in these last days to raise the standard! We have the answer for our city, our nation and the world. But the trumpet call of God commands us to warn of possible impediments to raising high the banners of Christ.

Raise High the Standard of Unity and Leadership

As Moses gathered the people of Israel together at the foot of Mount Sinai, he issued God's divine edict, "And ye shall be unto me a kingdom of priests, and an holy nation" (Ex. 19:6). Likewise, the call to the church issues forth: "Ye are a chosen generation, a royal priesthood, an holy nation, a peculiar people; that ye should show forth the praises of him who hath called you out of darkness into his marvellous light" (1 Pet. 2:9).

> **Warning!**
> **Discord and division give the enemy a foothold in our lives and our churches.**

The Banner of Unity

When the church in Acts prayed in one accord, the Holy Spirit fell on them with anointing and power, and they performed mighty signs and wonders (Acts 2:43). God's standard bearers need unity in their marriages, their families and their church if they are going to raise high the banner of unity.

The early church had all things in common (Acts 2:44). In these last days there will be persecution of God's people. But as we stand together under the banner of Jesus, the Bible promises us that the more we are persecuted, the more we will prosper and grow. God commands a blessing on us when we dwell together in unity (Psalm 133).

The device of the devil is to divide and then conquer. Every wall — racism, social status, denominational backgrounds, petty differences — that threaten to divide us must come down (Eph. 2:11-22). We have been fitted together by Christ to be the habitation of God through the Holy Spirit. We are one in Christ (Eph. 2:21-22; 4:1-6).

Blessing!
God commands His blessing upon those who raise high the standard of unity. He drives out the drought and sends a continual downpour of His Spirit.

God will raise up leaders among His standard bearers in whom the five-fold ministries — pastor, prophet, teacher, evangelist and apostle — are manifested. These servant-leaders will walk in the glory of God. Their hearts will be pure toward Him and compassionate for His people and the lost. The passion for leadership will be rekindled through repentance, refreshing and restoration. God desires leaders who will work together to follow His vision, call and direction and who will turn their backs on man-made plans and devices.

Warning!
God's people cannot lead according
to the standards of the world.
God's ways are not man's ways.

The Banner of Leadership

God calls His standard bearers to raise high the standard of leadership in the church. God's work will be done with excellence. No longer will His leaders be content with good ideas which originate in the world. No longer will they consider management by man's goals and objectives effective. No longer will they use mechanical irrigation to produce a season of rain. But, grounded in the Word of God, they will raise the standard of living in the church and the world (Phil. 4:8-9; Eph. 4:11-13).

Blessing!
Godly leaders who follow
Christ's example of servanthood
will equip the saints to take
the gospel into the world.

God will not tolerate leaders who use ministry for personal gain or popularity. He seeks men and women who hunger for His presence and cry out with David:

> Create in me a clean heart, O God; and renew a right spirit within me. Cast me not away from thy presence; and take not thy holy spirit from me. Restore unto me the joy of thy salvation; and

uphold me with thy free spirit. Then will I teach transgressors thy ways; and sinners shall be converted unto thee (Ps. 51:10-13).

Raise High the Standards of Courage and Praise

The Banner of Courage

God has not called us to walk around with our heads bowed in defeat. He has called us to subdue, conquer and win! Yes, the devil goes about as a roaring lion seeking whom he may devour (1 Pet. 5:8). But he cannot lay hold of the blood-washed, Holy Spirit-filled, anointed saints of God who are equipped and prepared for battle. When Jesus walked the cobblestone streets of Jerusalem, the religious leaders of His day desired to destroy Him. They seized hold of Him and dragged him to the brow of the hill just inside the city limits to throw Him to His death. But the Bible says, "But he passing through the midst of them went his way" (Luke 4:28-30).

Satan and his demonic underlords may try to entangle, ensnare and entrap you, but when they reach for you with their icy tentacles, they will get nothing but the banner of courage flying over your head!

God's command to us is not to lay in the lap of spiritual mediocrity but to march forth, storm the beach and possess the spiritual territory we are destined to claim.

Warning!
Be alert to the devices of the devil.
He seeks to steal and destroy from
ill-equipped and misinformed
standard bearers.

Godly men and women are being raised up for such a time as this (Esth. 4:13-14). It's time for war. It's time to go up and spoil the enemy. God is our great Commander-in-Chief, and with Him we are more than able to vanquish the adversary.

Blessing!
God infuses us with courage, the Word,
the name of Jesus and the power-filled
anointing of the Holy Spirit to defeat
the enemy and win the war!

The Banner of Praise

God inhabits the praises of His people (Ps. 22:3). The battle belongs to Him (1 Sam. 17:47). We cannot suppose that the kingdom of God will be ushered into this world without conflict or violence. Inner peace with God will bring us opposition from the powers and principalities which lord over this planet. Jesus came to bring not peace but a sword (Matt. 10:34). His kingdom suffers violence, and the violent take it by force (Matt. 11:12).

Warning!
We must never assume a fortress
mentality. A mere standoff with the
enemies of Christ is defeat.

We are not called to hold the fort. We are called to possess the land. Going into the world with the gospel brings constant persecution and attacks from the enemy. At times our circumstances will be dark and depressing, and our lives may seem dry, but we go forth as the morning. God's standard bearers praise Him before the battle (2 Chron. 20:21).

When we praise God in the midst of our trials, tribulations and tragedies, we experience His power, not our own, at work in our circumstances to bring certain victory. Our praise to God is a mighty weapon in His hand to defeat the enemy and release salvation, healing, deliverance — a spiritual flood in every area of our lives.

Blessing!
The praises of God open the door to
victory and close the door to the enemy.

It's time that the church closed the door once and for all on ungrateful and unthankful attitudes. We are supposed to be entering His courts with thanksgiving and praise (Ps. 100:4). Worship is more than a ritualistic exercise that motivates and inspires us. We need less perspiration and more inspiration; less performance and more humility; less irreverence and more respect for the Word of God; less apathy and more fear of God in our worship.

Worship brings us into His presence and drives out the enemy. Praise and worship must no longer be religious song services but a life completely dedicated and consecrated to God's sovereign purpose...this is our humble act of worship.

Raise High the Standard of Worship

The Banner of Relationship

The most important relationship we have in the church is with the Head of the church, Jesus Christ (Eph. 1:22-23). Our worship flows out of loving God with all of our heart, mind, soul and strength (Deut. 6:5; Matt. 22:37), but it must also lead us into righteous relationships with one another (Mic. 6:8). Every idol must be destroyed. Every roadblock which hinders our relationship with God and with one another must be destroyed (Eph. 2:13-22).

Warning!
As Christians we must destroy every
idolatrous thing or thought that
hinders worshiping God and Him alone.

Too much of the world has crept into our worship. We have become more concerned with our performance than His presence. We are seeking the gifts without the Giver. God seeks a church that is holy and separate from the world (Lev. 20:7; 2 Cor. 6:17). He wants a bride who is pure and blameless and who is prepared to meet the coming Bridegroom, Jesus Christ (Eph. 5:27).

Blessing!
A holy church who worships God in
spirit and in truth will discover His
presence in their everyday life.

The Banner of Sacrifice

As standard bearers we offer ourselves as living sacrifices to be used by Christ. When we refuse to be conformed to the world, our minds are renewed by the Word of God, and we become servants even as Jesus was the Suffering Servant on our behalf (Matt. 20:28; Mark 10:43-44; Rom. 12:1-2; Phil. 2:7-8). Our worship must be filled with the sweet incense of prayer and fasting as we proceed through the outer court of thanksgiving to the inner court of praise and into the holy of holies (Rev. 8:3-4).

Warning!
Standard bearers must never
seek status in sacrifice.

There will come a time in our worship when God's glory will so fill His church that it will be like the pillar of fire leading those enslaved out of Egypt into the promised land (Matt. 5:14-16). As we tabernacle with God (1 Cor. 6:19-20), we will be transformed from glory to glory (2 Cor. 3:18). As we look forth as the morning, fair as the moon, we will reflect His glory. Clear as the sun, we will be transparent for Christ. As terrible as an army marching with banners, we will raise high the standard of Jesus Christ in the world.

Blessing!
God will draw near to His standard
bearers and revive their souls with fresh
rain from heaven as they worship Him.

Raise High the Standards of Holiness and Devotion

Blow the trumpet in Zion (Joel 2:1). There are sinners in Zion. God's consuming fire will purge His standard bearers, and His baptizing fire will burn in their bones (Is. 33:14-16; Jer. 20:9).

The Banner of Holiness and Devotion

God's church faces this choice: compassion or compromise. We must choose today whom we will serve (Josh. 24:14-21). Holiness is separation and sanctification for God's purpose. His people cannot serve both God and man (Matt. 6:24). God seeks a radical, sold-out, totally committed people who will be to Him a holy nation and a royal priesthood, declaring His Word to the nations.

Warning!
The highway of holiness is narrow,
and few there are who walk thereon.
Cast down compromise and submit
to God's commands.

God is looking for sold-out, committed, devoted standard bearers who are dedicated to His cause at any price. We are not of those who shrink back in fear. We are faithful to pray, read the Bible, witness and go to church. We are marked out, distinguished by God as certain Christians and at the top of the devil's hit list.

Blessing!
Committed Christians will be able
to withstand Satan in times of turmoil
as well as in times of blessing.

Raise High the Standard of the Great Commission and the Blessed Hope

The Banner of the Great Commission

In Mark 16:15 Jesus said to his disciples, "Go ye into all the world, and preach the gospel to every creature." Our greatest call as standard bearers is to compel men to come to Christ. There is a world around us that is lost and dying without Jesus.

God gave my pastor, Dr. Lester Sumrall, a vision of the nations of the world plunging headlong into hell. His heart burned with passion for the lost, and his dream was to see one million people saved through his ministry before he went home to be with the Lord. Geana Tomlison from Florida was inspired by the description of this vision to write a song entitled "Win a Million":

Win A Million

Lying on my deathbed as a young and angry lad,
And there seemed no hope for me from the
sickness that I had.
All at once before my eyes, a decision to be
made:
On my one side was Your Holy Word, on the
other was my grave.

One night while I was praying, a picture came to
me.
There were people everywhere, as far as my eye
could see.
They were fallling off the edge of life into eternal
flames,
And as they approached their destiny, they were
crying out my name.

I closed my eyes more recently, and I beheld a
flood,
Flowing like a mighty river, and the content was
pure blood.
I sought to know its meaning, as deep called unto
deep.
'Twas the lives of the endtime harvesters, joining
hands to help me reap.

If I could live my life again, I would live it just the
same.
I'd run the race, I'd have kept the faith through
the power in Your name.
Through every trial I've overcome, every battle I
have won,
Just to see the smile on Your lovely face, and to
hear You say, "Well done."

Chorus:

Win a million — that's my vision from the Lord.
And my heart is filled with purpose — I've found
    what I was born for.
There's a world outside that's dying, as I come to
    You and pray,
I won't be satisfied, Lord Jesus, 'til I win a million
    every day.

In our own church I have personally witnessed 6,200 people give their lives to Jesus in a twelve-week period. Recently, God apprehended me to leave my church in Columbus, Ohio, and go to the war-ravaged country of Nicaragua to proclaim the message of repentance. Over twenty thousand men and women, boys and girls responded to the call of salvation. But this is not enough. We have got to go into *all* the world — our families, neighborhoods, businesses, cities and nation — and spread the good news of the gospel.

Warning!
Stop running to every "bless me" seminar!
Run to the streets, highways and byways
and compel men to come to Christ!

James 5:20 says, "Let him know, that he which converteth the sinner from the error of his way shall save a soul from death, and shall hide a multitude of sins."

Blessing!
The greatest joy in heaven will be
to meet someone who is there
as a result of your testimony.

The Banner of Hope

Jesus is coming. He is coming for a church who is eagerly looking for His appearing. Faster than the fleetest hoof ever struck pavement. Faster than the quickest bolt of lightning ever struck out of a dark-throated storm cloud. Jesus is coming.

Those chariots which haven't ridden the winds since Elijah are getting ready to carry the Son of God across eternity's skies to meet His bride. Jesus is preparing for His second advent onto this planet.

Blessing!
Jesus is coming for a church who
is patiently waiting for, watching for
and expecting Him.

The curtain on this final drama of humanity is not coming down; it is going up. The stage has been set, and we are the players. The last great revival is not coming; it is here! God has saved the best for last, and that includes you!

Jesus is coming soon! Comfort one another by proclaiming His imminent return (1 Thess. 5:1-11; Matt. 25:31). Take the gospel into all the world (Matt. 28:18-20; Mark 16:15). Declare Christ's righteousness and judgment. Serve the "least of these" in His name (Matt. 25:34-40). Tread upon serpents and take authority over the enemy (Mark 16:17-18; Luke 9:1,10:19-20).

Warning!
It is midnight prophetically.
We must work in the harvest fields
while there is still time because night
comes when no man can work.

Sound the Trumpet of Warning in Zion

Where is the church of Jesus Christ, the bride that God said He would come for who would look forth as the morning, fair as the moon, clear as the sun, and terrible as an army with banners? Where is this church?

This sleeping giant called the church is coming out of the shadows of the night. She is beginning to stir herself from her slumber. She is starting to properly respond to God, herself and her enemies. The church is recognizing her God-given armor and marching forth to take back everything that belongs to her.

The true battle lies within the heart and the soul of the church. The time has come to do battle. The time is now to put our flesh into submission and put the Spirit of holiness into action.

The future of our nation and the nations of the world lies not in the acts of politicians or governments, but in the actions of God's people. As God's people rise up in righteousness, the Spirit of God will invade every worldly arena and make spiritual demands upon those in leadership.

Now is the time to make our advance!

Now is the time to make our voice heard!

In 1858 a young Episcopalian preacher Dudley Tyng preached to five thousand men in a city-wide evangelistic meeting in Philadelphia. During the service one thousand gave their lives to Jesus Christ. Four days later Tyng died in a fatal accident. His dying words, as he lay thinking of the multitude just saved were, "Tell them to stand up for Jesus."

George Duffield preached the next Sunday on "Stand Therefore" from Ephesians 6:10-13. He also penned the words of the great hymn, "Stand Up For Jesus!" As we conclude this book, read these words, and determine to stand up for Jesus as a standard bearer in this final generation before the Bridegroom returns for His bride.

A Call to Warning

Stand up, stand up for Jesus,
  Ye soldiers of the cross,
Lift high His royal banner,
  It must not suffer loss;
From vict'ry unto vict'ry
  His army shall He lead,
Till ev'ry foe is vanquished,
  And Christ is Lord indeed.

Stand up, stand up for Jesus,
  The trumpet call obey;
Forth to the mighty conflict
  In this His glorious day.
Ye that are men now serve Him,
  Against unnumbered foes;
Let courage rise with danger,
  And strength to strength oppose.

Stand up, stand up for Jesus —
  Stand in His strength alone;
The arm of flesh will fail you —
  Ye dare not trust your own;
Put on the gospel armor,
  And watching unto prayer,
Where duty calls, or danger,
  Be never wanting there.

Stand up, stand up for Jesus
  The strife will not be long.
This day the noise of battle;
  The next the victor's song.
To him that overcometh,
  A crown of life shall be;
He with the King of Glory
  Shall reign eternally.[1]

181

To stand up for Jesus is God's divine call to us. This is no time to rest. This is the time for God's mighty army with banners to march forward and raise the standard. We are at war. The enemy has come in an onslaught to destroy families, marriages and children and withhold the torrential downpour of God's blessings in our lives. But the Bible says that it is getting ready to rain.

> Now is the time to let down your spiritual umbrella... to stand in the middle of your circumstance and allow the refreshing rain of God to fall upon you...the time has come for "No Dry Season!"

And it shall come to pass, if ye shall hearken diligently unto my commandments which I command you this day, to love the Lord your God, and to serve him with all your heart and with all your soul, That I will give you the rain of your land in his due season, the first rain and the latter rain, that thou mayest gather in thy corn, and thy wine, and thine oil (Deut. 11:13-14).

Now is the time to let down your spiritual umbrella. Now is the time to stand in the middle of your circumstance and allow the refreshing rain of God to fall upon you.

Are you ready to command the enemy to let go of your harvest? Are you ready to raise the standard of righteousness across this world? Are you ready to join myself and others on the most memorable march of eternity into the desert of your life?

A cloud is fast approaching over the horizon. The sound of thunder can be heard in the distance. The flash of lightning can be seen against the backdrop of a blackened sky. Rain is beginning to fall. The time has come for no dry season!

A Final Word

As I have read this manuscript through for the final time before it goes to print, my thoughts returned to the wandering warrior we met at the beginning of this book who was sojourning through the desert, desperately seeking to quench his thirst and cool his brow.

That warrior, worn and weather-beaten, now looks across the desert one last time. He stands at the edge of the rain forest. He has not succumbed to the heat of battle, to the blackness of night or to his parched surroundings. Instead, he has successfully navigated through the trials, tribulations and tragedies and found water for his weary soul once again.

I'm well aware that you could be that warrior. Now that you have read *No Dry Season!* I would like to share a final word with you and pray for you.

Close to your home,
   the wind is blowing,
      the fire is burning,
         the rain is falling.
            God is moving!

"But, Pastor Rod," you may protest. "If you only knew my heartache, my hurt, my pain and my past. If you only knew how dead the churches are around here. If you only knew the gossip, rejection, arrogance and pride that I have experienced from other Christians. Then you would understand why I am in a dry season and why at this moment I feel almost hopeless."

Oh, Standard Bearer, I *do* know what you face, and more important, your Commander understands.

But I also know and am fully persuaded that your Commander — Jesus Christ — is greater than your rejection and stronger than your tribulation. Jesus is greater than every circumstance that comes against you!

He is greater than your financial woes,
   health problems,
      family crises,
         church squabbles
            and all weapons formed against you.

Ye are of God, little children, and have overcome them: because greater is he that is in you, than he that is in the world (1 John 4:4).

When the enemy shall come in like a flood, the spirit of the Lord shall lift up a standard against him (Is. 59:19).

In closing, I want to pass on a word from the Lord to encourage you to lift over you His banner of love:

The greatest struggle you will face in being a standard bearer,
    in leaving your dry season,
        in coming into your season of refreshing,
            is you!

Within your soul are fortresses and strongholds that
    harbor your personal darknesses,
        hide your past shadows,
            hold on to your greatest failures
                and grasp your shattered dreams and hopes.

Before you can raise high His standard, before you can declare, "No Dry Season!"
    strongholds within you must be pulled down,
        vain imaginations must be crushed,
            poisonous thoughts must be shattered,
                and habits must be broken.

I have written this book to encourage you, to inspire you, to lift you up and to speak life into your heart. Hear God's word to you and declare it aloud, *No Dry Season!*

Now is the time to put this book down and take up the banner of the cross. Now is the time to examine yourself:

- What is in you that keeps living waters from flowing out of you?

- What is hindering the wellspring of God's Spirit from issuing forth out of you like a mighty river?

- What needs to be released from your past in order for you to receive all that God has for you in the present and the future?

What does your dry season signify? It means that God can and will intervene in the affairs of your everyday life and break up the hard, rocky soil of your heart so that His rain can soak deep to the root of your pain, guilt, hurt and suffering.

To the tormented mind, no dry season means deliverance.
To the troubled heart, no dry season means hope.
To the tortured body, no dry season means healing.

Do you hear the King calling you to no dry season? How will you respond?

Respond by praying:

> *King of kings, Commander and Captain of my soul, Lord Jesus, I declare to You that I will no longer look to the world as my source of supply. I determine in my heart to come out of the dry, parched desert of my circumstances into the refreshing rain of Your Spirit. I will live and prosper on the living water of Your Word. I will march into Your season of restoration and harvest. I proclaim that I will raise high Your standard and have no dry season until You return. Come quickly, Lord Jesus! Amen.*

Endnotes

Chapter 1
The Standard Has Been Passed On

1. Lester Sumrall as told to Tim Dudley, The Life Story of Lester Sumrall — the Man, the Ministry, the Vision (Green Forest, Ark.: New Leaf Press, 1993), 29-33.

Conclusion
A Call to Warning

1. Robert K. Brown and Mark R. Norton, *The One Year Book of Hymns* (Grand Rapids, Mich.: Tyndale House Publishers, Inc., 1995), June 9.

ABOUT THE AUTHOR

Rod Parsley began his ministry as an energetic nineteen-year old in the backyard of his parents' Ohio home. The fresh, "old-time gospel" approach of Parsley's delivery immediately attracted a hungry, God-seeking audience. From the seventeen people who attended that first 1977 backyard meeting, the crowds rapidly grew.

Today, as the pastor of Columbus, Ohio's 5,200-seat World Harvest Church, Parsley oversees World Harvest's preschool through grade twelve Christian Academy; World Harvest Bible College; Bridge of Hope missions and outreach; and *Breakthrough,* World Harvest Church's daily and weekly television broadcast. Parsley's message to "raise the standard" of spiritual intensity, moral integrity and physical purity not only extends across America but spans the globe, reaching throughout Canada and to nearly 150 nations via television and shortwave radio.

Thousands in arenas across the country and around the world can experience the saving, healing, delivering message of Jesus Christ as Parsley calls people back to Bible basics.

Rod Parsley currently resides in Pickerington, Ohio, with his lovely wife, Joni and their two beautiful children, Ashton and Austin.

Other Books by Rod Parsley

Ancient Wells — Living Water
The Backside of Calvary
Could It Be?
Daily Breakthrough
The Day Before Eternity
He Came First
No More Crumbs (Bestseller)
On the Brink (#1 Bestseller)
Repairers of the Breach

For information about Breakthrough, World Harvest Church, World Harvest Bible College, Harvet Preparatory School, or to receive a product list of the many books and CDs and DVDs by Rod Parsley write or call:

Breakthrough
P.O. Box 100
Columbus, Ohio 43216-0100
(800) 637-2288

World Harvest Bible College
P.O. Box 800
Columbus, Ohio 43216-0800
(800) 940-9422
www.worldharvestbiblecollege.org

Harvest Preparatory School
P.O. Box 32903
Columbus, OH 43232-0903
(614) 382-1111
www.harvestprep.org

If you need prayer, Breakthrough prayer warriors are ready to pray with you 24 hours a day, 7 days a week at:
(614) 837-3232

Visit Rod Parsley at his website address:
www.rodparsley.com